CAMBRIDGE LIBRARY COLLECTION

Books of enduring scholarly value

Cambridge

The city of Cambridge received its royal charter in 1201, having already been home to Britons, Romans and Anglo-Saxons for many centuries. Cambridge University was founded soon afterwards and celebrates its octocentenary in 2009. This series explores the history and influence of Cambridge as a centre of science, learning, and discovery, its contributions to national and global politics and culture, and its inevitable controversies and scandals.

Cambridge Retrospect

First published in 1943, T. R. Glover's reminiscences of his Cambridge world depict university life in the late nineteenth century. Looking back over the centuries of Cambridge, Glover describes how the university and its colleges first came into being – a result, he says, of 'the interplay of human needs, human passions and human hopes.' He recalls the colourful characters he met, from his tutor at St John's College – 'at once a terror and a delight' – to the many outstanding scholars and teachers who educated and influenced him. Glover captures the essence of undergraduate life as he knew it, which perhaps, as he says, had not fundamentally changed in three centuries. This book provides a fascinating glimpse into a previous age which will still resonate with the modern reader.

T0384636

Cambridge University Press has long been a pioneer in the reissuing of out-of-print titles from its own backlist, producing digital reprints of books that are still sought after by scholars and students but could not be reprinted economically using traditional technology. The Cambridge Library Collection extends this activity to a wider range of books which are still of importance to researchers and professionals, either for the source material they contain, or as landmarks in the history of their academic discipline.

Drawing from the world-renowned collections in the Cambridge University Library, and guided by the advice of experts in each subject area, Cambridge University Press is using state-of-the-art scanning machines in its own Printing House to capture the content of each book selected for inclusion. The files are processed to give a consistently clear, crisp image, and the books finished to the high quality standard for which the Press is recognised around the world. The latest print-on-demand technology ensures that the books will remain available indefinitely, and that orders for single or multiple copies can quickly be supplied.

The Cambridge Library Collection will bring back to life books of enduring scholarly value across a wide range of disciplines in the humanities and social sciences and in science and technology.

Cambridge Retrospect

Terrot Reaveley Glover

CAMBRIDGE
UNIVERSITY PRESS

CAMBRIDGE UNIVERSITY PRESS

Cambridge New York Melbourne Madrid Cape Town Singapore São Paolo Delhi

Published in the United States of America by Cambridge University Press, New York

www.cambridge.org
Information on this title: www.cambridge.org/9781108002561

© in this compilation Cambridge University Press 2009

This edition first published 1943
This digitally printed version 2009

ISBN 978-1-108-00256-1

CAMBRIDGE RETROSPECT

CAMBRIDGE
UNIVERSITY PRESS
LONDON: BENTLEY HOUSE
NEW YORK   TORONTO   BOMBAY
CALCUTTA   MADRAS: MACMILLAN

PETER MASON
From the painting by Charles Brock

CAMBRIDGE RETROSPECT

BY

T. R. GLOVER

CAMBRIDGE

AT THE UNIVERSITY PRESS

1943

To

E. A. BENIANS
MASTER OF ST JOHN'S COLLEGE

CONTENTS

PLATES

Thanks are expressed to the Council of St John's College for permission to reproduce these three portraits.

Des a man, honey. Dat's all. Dat's all I knows—des wunner dese yer mans w'at you see trollopin 'roun' eve'y day. Nobody ain't never year w'at his name is.

UNCLE REMUS

Let not Ambition mock their useful toil.

THOMAS GRAY

PREFACE

People work at Colleges in different ways. The Junior Bursar, as we call him at St John's—he may have other titles elsewhere—thinks of a College as a series of buildings, where roofs leak and taps freeze, and undergraduates complain of the bath system. The Steward thinks of a kitchen, a dinner committee of young men, a suggestion-book, cooks and commissariat. The Senior Bursar of St John's has written a valuable financial history of the College. Tutors live upon University regulations, the *Reporter* and the *Ordinances*, and think of examinations. Of all these things nothing will be found in this book; it cannot be used as a substitute for the *Ordinances*.

Πόλις γὰρ ἄνδρες—so I read in the first play of Aeschylus with which I wrestled as a schoolboy. If a state is to be thought of not as a series of monuments, trivial or magnificent, nor as a constitution, but as a human society of kindred blood and kindred aims, something of the same sort is true of a College; and that is the theme of this book. Perhaps—for I have friends across the Atlantic—my little book will cross the Ocean; and over there there may be those who will be ready to read in briefest outline (but, I hope, not without a human interest) how the University and its Colleges came into being as the result of the interplay of human needs, human passions and human hopes. Human contacts are still the main feature of College life; and some chapters try to describe that life. Lastly from 'documents' (what a big word for nonsense in *The Granta*!) an attempt is made to illustrate undergraduate life, as I knew it half a century ago; and perhaps it has not essentially changed yet. Those who read the Gawdy letters (see pages 26–28) will perhaps think it has not fundamentally changed in three centuries. Who would have wished it to change —this splendid union of youth and College—ἡβᾶν μετὰ τῶν φίλων?

I have said that many of the quotations in Chapter VI come from *The Granta*—from the first five or six volumes of it, one excepted which some visitor had borrowed. Some of the more vigorous verses were clearly written by R. C. Lehmann, the genial and robust 'Rudie Lehmann', rowing man and Liberal M.P., and author of the delightful *Harry Fludyer*, which might well be re-published. (Rumour said he got his mother to write Harry's mother's letters; I hope it is true.) But at least two poems quoted come from an in-College source, a MS. magazine. Thus: about 1890 Cameron Waller (long since a Professor at London, Ontario) got a College reading-room established, complete with suggestion-book. Suggestions grew so fast and furious that Waller suppressed the book. Its place was at once taken by 'The Licensed Wallerer's Gazette', the work chiefly of R. H. Forster and 'Bally' Harris. Later on pieces from this were printed with the odd title *Washings from the Wallerer*. (I know the origin of this title, but, like Herodotus, I do not mention it.)

This work contained J. J. Alexander's verses, quoted on pages 123 and 124, the tutor's testimonial (with the motto from *Paradise Lost*, Book II, 'Others apart sat on a HILL retired') and *De Disgustibus*. I should say that I was told as a freshman that Lady Margaret had bequeathed to the College a million tons of bottled gooseberries, which we were still in the late 'eighties working through. The reader may think this improbable; it seemed more credible at the time than he might imagine; but see Alexander's poem. It was not his only contribution to *The Wallerer* on the dinner question. The cook of the period was a Mr Cash; hence the statement of C. A. M. Pond (afterwards a Professor in New Zealand) in *The Wallerer* that Lady Margaret had left Cash to found the College, for which purpose he had invented his celebrated pie-crust. That perhaps passed; but when Alexander parodied Cowper's 'Toll for the brave'—

> Toll for the cow,
> The cow that is no more;
> She is an angel now;
> Her age was forty-four,

with other less plaintive verses, 'the rustle of the writ was heard in the land'; and the whole affair went to the College Council who discouraged writs and made peace. It was said that, when the *Washings* went before the Council, Professor Mayor was heard to ejaculate: 'Shade of Aristophanes! is this wit?' He had stumbled on a couplet in a 'Johnian Topsy-turveydom'—

> The Junior Dean was heard to swear,
> And steaks rejoiced Professor Mayor.

The Junior Dean was Alfred Caldecott, who perhaps did not himself as a rule swear, but he made others swear, virtuous and sinful alike, everybody; *qui facit per alium....*

The first reading room is now incorporated in the College Library—the pitch-pine portion. The next was the so-called 'Old Music Room', which R. F. Scott used to say he once visited. One undergraduate was in the room, who at once went out. By and by another came in, and looked at Scott, as if Scott ought to have known that it was etiquette for only one man to read the papers at one time; so Scott went out, he said. The modern reading room is larger and better, and its furniture (bought with W. A. Cox's bequest) is more modern still—none of my choosing. But there is little tangible in College to recall me—a handle on a door I would claim. No great monument that! you say; but consider.

A suggestion involving expenditure of £1000 would at once have stirred the imagination of the Junior Bursar of that day; it was a feat indeed to get him to do something that cost less than nine-pence. I find in fifty-five years that things are forgotten in College—things and people. Let me drift back, however, to my proper task, the past and the people of the past; and add that in the case of nearly everybody I have mentioned—*nearly* every-body—I would say with Dr Johnson

Yet still he fills affection's eye.

T. R. G.

February 1943

Chapter I

ORIGINS

I

It might be a question how far back a Retrospect should extend; and one or two answers might be given. For instance, perhaps the first reference to Cambridge in extant literature is in the Venerable Bede's *Ecclesiastical History* (iv, 19). Stone is sought to make a coffin for Queen Aethelthryth or Etheldreda, who had died an abbess at Ely. The district of Ely, says Bede, is on every side encompassed with water and marshes and has no large stones; but the brothers sent on this errand came to 'a small deserted city' (*civitatula*) 'which in the language of the English is called Grantacaestir', and near its walls they found a white marble coffin, beautifully wrought, with a lid of the same stone. Grantchester, say the annotators; probably not, say the antiquaries, suggesting that it is more likely to have been Chesterton.[1] But, whichever it was, the archaeologists would carry our retrospect much further back. Mr Cyril Fox, in his *Archaeology of the Cambridge Region*, dates the bronze age in this area about 2000 B.C. He assembles an extraordinary mass of material of successive periods and races, to which the reader is referred with confidence. The retrospect of an ordinary member of the University may not improperly be limited at times to the academic story.

Accordingly, we note in the year 1209 a large body of men on Madingley Hill looking in our direction—men footsore and weary, we can well believe, for they have tramped from Oxford, a distance of eighty miles. At whatever rate the 'well-girt man' of Herodotus could have got over the ground, it may not be a bad guess that this body of straggling students, launched into the

[1] See A. Gray, *The Town of Cambridge*, pp. 1-2.

sudden expedition, took a week before they looked down on the little medieval town they sought. Needless to say, it had not then the architectural features that we pick out to-day from the hill. But they had reached their intended goal, and the next thing was to find quarters for the night, and to make plans for food and shelter and some kind of lecture-rooms for the months and years that lay before them. It is interesting to note how the commonplace and the humdrum treads on the heels of adventure. In old days people would talk (and perhaps feel) sentimentally about the emigrant sailing from Liverpool. He at least had a dream of a new land, a new freedom and fresh prosperity; but when the Ocean was crossed and he had sailed up the St Lawrence, he would disembark at Levis, opposite Quebec, in an immigrant shed among inspectors, to be herded with others into a train which should take him in several days to the North-West and the prairie. We need not follow him so far; Levis is dismal enough and the French inspectors no sentimentalists where the British immigrant is concerned. Some hundred of students to be fitted into a new town —old, no doubt it thought itself, old and shabby many of its houses, but new to them; and the problems that faced them were both old and new—the age-long problem of food and how to pay for it, and the perennial problem of what we call College life— what to do with your students, when they are not in the lecture-room listening to a lecturer or wishing he would stop. What will they do, when they get outside? And there we touch discipline, and in a moment learn why they had come. When Alice (through the Looking Glass) is in talk with the White Queen, she notices that the royal lady keeps murmuring to herself, and makes out that the words are 'Bread and butter'—rather surprising words on a Queen's lips, one might say; but she was a human soul, and she touches there one of the fundamental problems of University life. When we reach the married don some centuries later, we shall find again the bearing of this problem on College life. Learning, idealism, the development of character in a natural married life— so forth; and the married man's problem of the cost of a family—

food, roof, clothing, they are the medieval requisites; and the problem of the College is whether it can get, or keep, a real teacher for a hack's wage. This is lowly matter, but royal commissions have been needed to solve the questions. Thus one thread at least runs through the fabric of University life from the beginning till to-day.

But let us see why these men came here.

II

'Town and gown rows' hardly suggest glory to-day, but it is a curious thing that from conflicts so essentially inglorious have come some of the greatest extensions of learning. Legend says otherwise; for, as Professor Maitland wittily put it, 'the oldest of all inter-university sports was a lying match. Oxford was founded by Mempricius in the days of Samuel the prophet, and Cambridge by the Spanish Cantaber in the days of Gurguntius Brabtruc.'[1] But in 1209 a scholar of Oxford killed a woman of Oxford—it was of course accidental, as, it is commonly told us, such episodes are apt to be; but the Mayor and burgesses resented it after the manner of 'townees'. They made a raid on the hall or lodgings of the unlucky student, and seized a number of 'clerks'; some of whom, two or three, they put to death, with the consent of King John, who was at the time quarrelling with Pope and Bishops. And once again, as so often in University history, it was affirmed that innocent men suffered ; they are easier to arrest and perjury is not a difficult art. A great migration of Masters and scholars followed—3000 of them, Matthew Paris says, 'and', wrote Rashdall, 'there is no reason to suspect that estimate of more than the usual medieval exaggeration'. What with the migration and the Papal Interdict, the existence of the University of Oxford was practically suspended, till peace was made in 1214, and the citizens of Oxford properly humbled in penance and finance. The de-

1 Maitland, *Township and Borough*, p. 51. Spenser speaks of Cambridge as the 'elder sister'.

parting students went to Reading, to Paris and to Cambridge, and that is the first historical record of our University.

'What attracted them to that distant marsh town, we know not', wrote the Oxford historian in his youth. A modern founder, if he were confined to the neighbourhood, would surely prefer Royston Heath or Newmarket.

Coleridge, as an undergraduate in February 1792, writes of 'the quiet ugliness of Cambridge'. ''Tis a dismally flat country, Sir,' said Robert Hall, the great preacher,[1] 'dismally flat....Before I came to Cambridge, I had read in the prize poems, and in some other works of fancy, of "the banks of the Cam", of "the sweetly flowing stream", and so on; but when I arrived here, I was sadly disappointed. When I first saw the river, as I passed over King's College bridge, I could not help exclaiming, Why, the river is standing still to see people drown themselves! and that, I am sorry to say, is a permanent feeling with me.... Shocking place for the spirits, Sir.... Were you ever at Bristol, Sir? There is scenery, scenery worth looking upon and worth thinking of.' He had, no doubt, the Avon Gorge in mind. And on his last visit, he said much the same, but magnanimously added: 'I always say of my Cambridge friends, when I witness their contentedness in such a country, "Herein is the faith and patience of the saints".'[2]

A similar impression was made on the American, Mr Everett, who was a student at Cambridge from 1859 to 1864 and wrote one of the outstanding books upon it.[3] 'Cambridge is of all provincial boroughs the most insignificant, the dullest and the ugliest. It is at once the last town on the chalk, and the first on the fen,—a combination admirable for raising wheat, but wholly at variance with beauty of all kinds. An endless expanse of marsh, cut up by long-drawn reaches of sluggish brooks, bordered with pollard

1 *Works of Robert Hall*, vi, p. 42.
2 Defoe in 1722 pitied the people who live in the fogs of Cambridgeshire, but remarked that they live unconcerned and as healthy as other people, except for ague.
3 Everett, *On the Cam*, p. 9. Very similar is the description of Mr Bristed, *Five Years in an English University*, p. 13.

willows and unhappy poplars, form the prospect of the lowlands.'
The Gogmagogs he dismisses as a slope or a molework; 'and
through the melancholy of these marshes creeps what seems a forgotten canal, nowhere over seventy feet wide, with a few locks
and half a hundred black barges;[1] and this you are informed is the
river Cam'. Cambridge 'seems to have stagnated for three hundred years.... Its streets are too crooked to be convenient or im-
posing, and not crooked enough to be picturesque. The buildings
are mostly of bricks baked of the local clay, which is of a dirty
white, relieved by occasional touches of dingy red'—made worse,
he adds, by the combination of smoke with the condensations of
the marsh fog.

Dismal as these men, thinking of the Don and the Hudson and
Devonshire, found the flat scene, and the uncomfortable climate
with its damps and cramps—to say nothing for the moment of
harsh judgments of the natives, to which we shall have to return,
it is to be borne in mind that to others Cambridgeshire has made
a very different appeal. Charles Kingsley wrote glowing vindica-
tions of the fens, and the bird-lover of to-day will not hear a word
against them. And the town, too—of course, it has changed in
seven centuries—has found people to love it and to say so with
something of a lyric note. Amy Levy, authoress of that remarkable Jewish novel *Reuben Sachs* (which after half a century will
bear re-reading), wrote:

> Oh, fairest of all fair places.
>   Oh, sweetest of all old towns,
> With the birds, and the greenness and greyness,
>   And the men in caps and gowns.[2]

And here are other verses by Kitty Coates:

> From north and south the counties
>   With hills and splendour call;
> But Cambridgeshire of fenlands
>   Is gentlest of them all!

1 On the barges, see Mr Clark; Atkinson and Clark, *Cambridge Described
and Illustrated*, p. xxv; 'laden with coal, or heaped high with turf and sedge'.
2 Quoted from memory, as the printed source is beyond me.

Sweetness of cool gray beanfields,
   May in the snow-white hedge,
And amber trail of sunsets
   Against the ploughed land's edge.

Open, and green, and golden
   It spreads before the eyes,
With roads that call to follow,
   White under quiet skies.

And under dreaming willows
   The river winds and gleams,
Nor speaks above a whisper
   For fear to break their dreams.

III

But Mr Everett's description touches one or two points which
explain the history of the town and the choice of it for the home
of a University. Cambridge is, as he says, close upon the fens;
and the Cam was, he says, a river with half a hundred black barges.
In the middle ages, when the choice of the site was made, Lincoln,
Peterborough, and Cambridge had as good a right to be reckoned
seaside towns as has Lynn to-day.[1] In its earlier days Cambridge
was a military headquarters of the Danish invaders, who came up
the river from the Wash, though the Castle Hill was perhaps made
as a defence against them.[2] The fens were very navigable, though
the water was not salt nor its flow continuous. Northward of
Cambridge they stretched to Lincoln. Southward or to the
South-East, not very far away, lies a range of hills, between 250
and 500 feet high, that form a little watershed for the small rivers
of East Anglia. Between hill and fen is a belt of level country,
more or less dry—at least out of the water—and the river. Out
of the water—for St·John's, we used to be told, is twenty feet

1 Bp Creighton, *Historical Essays*, p. 266. Cf. A. Gray, *Cambridge and its story*, p. 29.
2 Atkinson and Clark, p. 5.

above the sea. Old Roman and Saxon roads cross a little above the town—the Icknield Way and Ermine Street. We learn, too, that in the middle ages East Anglia was one of the most densely populated parts of England[1]—if 'densely' may be given a comparative rather than a positive sense. Here then we have the elements for a town of consequence—population—plenty of food and fuel from the fens, which swarmed with wild life, beast, bird, and fish of species not all to be found to-day—oversea goods from Lynn—a junction of great roads—a river, a bridge,[2] and a sea-front of a sort. Ships were smaller and of far less draught than to-day, and the Wash and the Cam gave one of the best inlets and outlets for trade with Europe. The great roads connected the place easily with the North, and rather less directly with London; and it became a 'natural emporium', the seat of four of the annual fairs at which much of the trade of the middle ages was carried on, while one of the most famous, Stourbridge Fair, was held just outside the town.[3] Here Oxford bought her salted eels for Lent; and wool and woollens changed hands.[4] A place of commerce where men gathered naturally,[5] a place easy of access, and well supplied with food, it was not so bad a spot for a University, perhaps; at all events a very similar combination of advantages has in our own day made great University centres in the New World, and more recently in the English provinces. Centuries after the great migration from Oxford, we find George Herbert the poet, as Public Orator of the University, thanking King James I for stopping the drainage of the fens by certain bold speculators; for town and gown both held that the reclamation would leave Cambridge 'high and dry' as we say, stripped of its chief means of communi-

1 A. Gray, p. 19.
2 The name Cam does not appear till about 1600, and comes from the corruption of the town's name Grantabrigge to Cantabrige and Cambridge.
3 It has been suggested that Bunyan modelled Vanity Fair on Stourbridge.
4 Forbes and Ashford, *Our Waterways*, p. 45.
5 Further evidence of its commercial significance has been found in the existence of a Jewry in Cambridge, Conybeare, *History of Cambridgeshire*, p. 117.

cation with the sea and the world; and in that case 'the beautiful dwellings of the Muses' would become 'like worn-out widows or sapless withered logs'. So perhaps the choice of the marsh town was not so very out-of-the-way after all.

Cambridge, then, like Oxford and Paris and Bologna, owes its foundation to no external authority, neither to Church or State, nor Pope or King. It is the creation of a race of students, turbulent and disorderly no doubt, but bent on learning.[1] The early history of the new University is not unlike that of the others. In 1229 there was another of those fierce town and gown rows—'savage, sanguinary, devastating conflicts'[2]—at Paris this time; and Cambridge reaped the benefit once more. Ten years later there was another at Oxford, but this time the students went off to Northampton, which for a quarter of a century could boast, more or less, a University of its own. In 1260 another fight with townspeople sent a lot of Cambridge scholars to Northampton, and more followed for the same reason in 1263 from Oxford. In 1264 Henry III besieged Northampton; the scholars played a vigorous part in the defence, and narrowly escaped hanging when the town fell, betrayed by the monks. A short while after, a writ in the King's name decreed the 'entire cessation of the University of Northampton'.

IV

So that danger to Cambridge was averted, but the townspeople remained. At the time of the Peasants' Rising, in April 1381, the townsmen broke into the University Church and burnt charters and muniments; and so well pleased with themselves were they, that they did it again in June—one old woman, Margaret Starre, being conspicuous in the Market as she flung the ashes from the fire into the air, crying: 'Away with the learning of the clerks! away with it!'[3] Turbulence, then, we are told, was one of the

---

1 A. J. Carlyle in *Progress and History*, p. 86.
2 Bp Lightfoot's description.   3 Powell, *Peasant Rising*, p. 50.

characteristics of the medieval student; and it is interesting to
learn that in 1413 Parliament expelled the Irish on this ground
from the English Universities, unless they could prove that they
were subjects of the English King.

Two great movements mark the medieval history of the University—the struggle for independence and the rise of Colleges.
Neither 'University' nor 'College' is originally a word with any
suggestion of learning or teaching; they both mean 'corporation'
or 'society'. It is only the success with which teachers and students
have grouped themselves into societies and maintained themselves
in growing independence and self-government, that has at last
given 'University' and 'College' their exclusive suggestion of
places of learning. The teaching and training institutions of to-day,
created and controlled perhaps by Town Councils, are in the strict
and original sense of the words neither 'Colleges' nor 'Universities'. One of the early endeavours of the University—and
we may some day see it again in the new foundations—was for
independence of the town and then for some control of it. Many
an undergraduate to-day has an uneasy feeling, perhaps instilled at
home, that the town shopkeepers will cheat him if they can;[1]
hospes and *hostis*, certain old Latinists told us, looked too much
alike. Chaucer, in the Reve's scandalous tale, shows us the Miller
of Trumpington over-reaching the two young clerks with
Northern accents, and then more than paid back by them. It was
in the interests of the town to have students; but, as we see in
modern labour disputes, identity of interest means also divergence
of interest. This appeared in Cambridge; and when the town passed
a certain point in systematically over-charging the scholars for
their lodging and their food, two things followed, reminders of
which we see to this day in the College buildings of Cambridge

1 The late Mr Schiller-Szinessy, Reader in Rabbinic at Cambridge, is
responsible for the statement that Pumbaditha was one of the great Universities of the ancient East; 'so that through all the East it was a proverb
that there were no such thieves as the greengrocers of Pumbaditha'. The
oriental student was perhaps more vegetarian than ours.

and in the old habit of selling butter by the yard.[1] The University organized itself and did so for self-defence against various enemies —the tradesmen and lodging-house-keepers to begin with; and, once organized, it was able to fix the prices of food for the scholars and to deal with the question of lodgings. The secession to Northampton helped that matter forward. By 1278 the town complained to King Edward I that the University on its own authority is actually requiring the town bailiffs to make corporal oath of submission to the Chancellor and Masters.[2] The years 1314 and 1383 mark big stages of the extension of the Chancellor's jurisdiction in cases where scholars were concerned.[3] Reference to the Crown would appear to have been a strong line with the University. Oxford has a similar tale to tell, and its historian[4] sums it up by saying that 'by the middle of the fifteenth century the Town had been crushed and was almost entirely subjugated to the authority of the University. The burghers lived henceforth in their own town almost as helots or subjects of a conquering people.' Cambridge, we read, was slower in achieving its freedom; but then, we are told, Cambridge is apt to be a little behind Oxford, as (and here the historians grew lyrical) befits a younger sister.[5] Now and then, it is true, as at the Reformation and in the modern study of Natural Sciences, Cambridge has for a little taken the lead, but the common belief seems to be that its role is to follow. The public press is more generally manned by Oxford.

Side by side with the battle for freedom from town rule went on another for liberty from ecclesiastical control. There were friars to deal with, who wanted degrees on their own terms— great monastic houses at Barnwell and elsewhere—and a Bishop

1 It is perhaps of interest that the yard measure for butter is still handed over to each new Senior Proctor on entering upon his office. We always had so many inches of butter when I was young; 'the dear old lubricant of my youth', said Heitland, 'butter by inches'.
2 A. Gray, p. 27.
3 Rashdall, *Universities of Europe*, ii, p. 548.
4 So Rashdall, and J. R. Green, *Oxford Studies*, p. 4.
5 See the reference to Spenser on p. 3 note.

at Ely. Up to the end of the fourteenth century the Bishop would decide disputes in the University faculties and hear appeals from the Chancellor's decisions; but slowly progress was made towards freedom from episcopal control. In 1401 the Pope, Boniface IX, dispensed with the episcopal confirmation for the election of a Chancellor. In 1430 the Chancellor-elect, John of Dunwich, refused the oath of obedience to the Bishop, and a law-suit followed before Papal delegates, sitting in the Chapterhouse of Barnwell, in 1432. One of the documents produced for the Chancellor was an alleged Papal bull of the year 624, in which the Pope, Honorius I, declaring himself a former student at Cambridge, confers on the University exemption from all authority of bishop or archbishop. The delegates decided in favour of the Chancellor—a decision of more permanent value than the documents on which it was based. Two hundred years before the Bishop had been a safeguard from the Sheriff;[1] now he goes; and the Pope's turn is coming.[2]

Meanwhile the other great movement toward the College system was in progress. Without Colleges the medieval University was naturally not very like the one we know, and its students had different loyalties, and different habits of life. They came from anywhere and everywhere—wandering, begging and fighting. Sometimes a 'fetcher' went round a district and brought in a batch together. Sometimes, as we have seen, a body would migrate from another University. The student, travelling to or from his University, was often exempted from the prohibition against carrying arms. When he reached his destination he still kept them; John Major the Scot says the Cambridge student carried sword and bow.[3] Almost the only organization available to help him was his 'Nation'. The 'Nations' were loose groups, based on a man's birthplace North or South of such and such a

1 A. Gray, p. 25.
2 H. W. C. Davis, *England under the Normans*, p. 501, the opposition of the University to Papal interference.
3 A. Gray, p. 110; Major's visit would be about 1490.

line, and the like. 'Nations' are long extinct in Cambridge—dying, one supposes, a natural death as better systems of group-life arose; but they survive in the Scottish Universities and bear a part in every Rectorial election. Whatever other end they served in medieval times, they must have been available for purposes of faction; and faction-fighting was perhaps the only efficient form of athletics then known. Games with bats and balls were discouraged as 'insolent'. Brawls and fights were no monopoly of freshmen; for we read of Masters of Arts, monks and friars and beneficed clergy, and even Heads of Colleges, taking part in them;[1] and Cambridge has a story of an ex-Mayor wanting to fight a Chancellor with his fists.[2] Disorder is the great feature—quarrels with townees about food, lodging and a hundred other things; and then the beginnings of order slowly appear. Some grouping of men is required for guidance, for safety, for health, for instruction; and in turn we find the Master, the Hostel and the College emerge.

V

First comes the Master. The degree originally was a technical admission to the status and privileges of a teacher. The first and most obvious basis of union was attendance on the same Master, as in Athens hundreds of years before. By and by we find Masters in charge of hostels.[3] The Master, with certain guarantees, took a house and lodged students along with himself and under his control. The students paid him for their board, but were not necessarily taught by him. It was a system of lodging-houses, and it lasted long—only in fact dying out when the Colleges, which were a later invention, extended their first plan and took in 'pensioners', or paying students in addition to scholars 'on the foundation'. John Caius enumerates eighteen, the last dropping out in 1562. The hostels, if shorter-lived, were very much more

1 Rashdall, ii, p. 415.   2 Cooper, *Annals*, i, p. 164.
3 A. Gray, pp. 24, 25.

numerous than the Colleges, and some of them were large—as large as a good-sized College perhaps. Dr Venn[1] says there is little doubt that in some respects the hostels occupied the primary place in public estimation, for it was to them rather than to the Colleges that any young men of rank would go who came to Cambridge at all. The great monasteries by wealth of endowment and splendour of building overshadowed both Colleges and hostels. The libraries and the churches belonged to the monks, and those were days when books were costly. The Clerk of Oxenford in the *Canterbury Tales* had but little gold in his coffer, for all he got he spent on books and learning:

> For him was lever have at his beddes heed
> Twenty bokes, clad in blak or reed,
> Of Aristotle and his philosophye
> Than robes riche, or fithele, or gay sautrye.

When we learn that his twenty books must have cost him as much as the value of three average citizens' houses in a great town,[2] we can believe he had little gold, and we can understand better the difficulties of the poor student of medieval Cambridge. The hostels then, like the Colleges still later, must have been marvellously uncomfortable—worse perhaps than the quarters of modern students in an Indian University. The houses were cold, dark and dirty, the windows without glass, the fires without chimney, and the earth for floor unboarded.[3] (Within living memory there were rooms, perhaps there still are, in our old Colleges, with the floor lying immediately on the soil.) Outside, the narrow streets were all smell and dirt;[4] but men were used to such conditions.

1 John Venn, *Early Collegiate Life*, p. 42.
2 Coulton, *Chaucer and his England*, p. 99.
3 Coulton, *Chaucer and his England*, pp. 83 ff. and for later period Venn, *Early Collegiate Life*.
4 Maitland, *Township and Borough*, p. 69. Rashdall, ii, p. 388. Atkinson and Clark, p. 40, a vigorous passage from an Act of Parliament, 35 Henry VIII. Coulton, *Chaucer and his England*, p. 267: 'The first Sanitation Act for England was that of the Parliament held at Cambridge in 1388, and is generally attributed to the filth of that ancient borough.'

Clean streets are a modern endeavour, not yet wholly achieved, as we know in this dog-infested Cambridge.

At the end of the thirteenth century there was a Bishop of Ely with ideas. As bishop, he was patron and visitor of a Hospital of St John in Cambridge, and he thought it possible that, as well as the poor and the sick, the Hospital might house 'studious scholars living after the rule of the scholars in Oxford called of Merton'. He obtained letters patent from King Edward I to permit his plan being tried. But it failed; and then the bishop transferred his scholars to two houses next the church of St Peter, outside the Trumpington Gate, and gave them a small endowment. This was in March 1284. Two years later he died before completing his design; but, by what he did, Hugo de Balsham had inaugurated a new era. He had *not* founded a College, or a place of teaching; but he had endowed a hostel and thereby given it a permanent character, which no hostel had yet had; and, further, all its residents were maintained by the endowment; it was not a speculation nor a joint venture.[1] And moreover it was a secular foundation. It was not furnished with costly buildings; for the collegiate system was still an experiment.[2] For the church of St Peter the new body had forever to pay twenty shillings a year to St John's Hospital; and to this day Peterhouse pays its pound to St John's.[3]

The next great stage is marked by Clare Hall and its statutes of 1359. This was a College, and it was to consist of a Master and nineteen Fellows (*socii* not *scholares*)—the Master to be elected by the Fellows, and he and they to fill vacancies in their ranks—and in addition ten poor scholars were to be maintained on the foundation and to study singing, grammar and logic.[4] One curious clause in the statutes requires one or two Fellows every night to examine the scholars' rooms to prevent their assembling 'to eat or to talk', and the fines on 'confabulants' are to go to the Fellows' Commons.[5] A clause of larger spirit enacts that the Fellowships

1 A. Gray, pp. 32–7.   2 Atkinson and Clark, p. xxxiii.
3 Mullinger, *St John's College*, p. 4.   4 A. Gray, p. 44.
5 J. Peile, *Christ's College*, p. 17.

shall be open to men of all nationalities and to graduates of other Universities[1]—a remarkable instance of the feeling that a University's function is to 'put men at a universal point of view'. The origin of the Colleges is thus not monastic—rather, as Bishop Lightfoot said, *anti*-monastic—though houses for their student members were founded by the great orders.[2]

VI

But now a change was to come, and in a curious way. The greatest Oxford name in the medieval period is Wiclif's; he was the Master of Balliol, he resided, he lectured, and he taught Oxford to think along new lines—lines so strong that Oxford grew to be more thoroughly national than ever before,[3] but so new that the whole place became suspect to the old-fashioned and the well-established. Cambridge, as Dr Rashdall says,[4] 'came into fashion with cautious parents and attracted the patronage of Royal champions of orthodoxy and their ecclesiastical advisers', and to this we owe four Colleges of the fifteenth century—King's in particular (1440). For King's is the foundation of Henry VI, and suspicion is written in its statutes. It is not at Oxford; but, though it was at Cambridge, for centuries it was not of Cambridge; it was 'an Oxford *enclave* at Cambridge',[5] so independent of the University, the Chancellor and the Masters, that till the nineteenth century members of King's maintained the right to University degrees without University examination. The College is beautiful—

> They dreamt not of a perishable home
> Who thus could build. Be mine, in hours of fear
> Or grovelling thought, to seek a refuge here,

1 A. Gray, p. 44, who notes that in the Pembroke statutes of about the same date students of French birth who have studied at an English University are given preference.
2 *Hist. Essays*; cf. J. W. Clark in Atkinson and Clark, p. xxxvii: 'The whole collegiate system was intended to counteract monastic influence.'
3 T. F. Tout, *Political History*, iii, pp. 424–5.
4 Rashdall, ii, p. 553.   5 A. Gray, p. 66.

wrote Wordsworth of the Chapel in a famous sonnet; and in another as famous he compares the beauty and the music of the place to

> Thoughts whose very sweetness yieldeth proof
> That they were born for immortality.[1]

But the King's scheme was curious and awkward. To find the place for his College, he cleared the town and its wharves from the river bank, making meadows of the busiest part of medieval Cambridge; and then for close on three centuries his Chapel stood alone amid grass and sheep, waiting for the College buildings till 1724.[2] Still the scheme, long unfinished as it was—for the Chapel itself had to be completed by Henry VIII—marks a new era in Colleges; magnificence of architecture was a new thing here.

The sixteenth century saw a still greater revolution in the fortunes and fame of Cambridge. At the beginning the poet Lydgate says, complacently,

> Of heresie Cambridge had never blame.

The early years of this century saw Cambridge the very centre and heart of the Reformation movement; the middle years saw it furnish Queen Mary with a large proportion of her more significant martyrs; and in the long reign of Elizabeth the ascendancy of Cambridge over Oxford is still more marked. All but one of Elizabeth's Archbishops of Canterbury were Cambridge men, so were the outstanding Puritans and Separatists; and the poets, the scholars and the statesmen—a Spenser, an Ascham, Cecils and Bacons—were of Cambridge, too[3]—the men who brought England through the great crisis of political, intellectual and religious rebirth.

1 A. Gray, p. 72.

2 Everett, *On the Cam*, p. 120, has an almost rhapsodic passage on the Chapel: 'Every child of Cambridge walks in delight before its peerless beauty by day, and trembles in its awful shadow at night....'—'the fairest temple in England.'

3 A. F. Pollard, *Pol. Hist.* vi, p. 444; Lightfoot, *Hist. Essays*, p. 156.

Oxford had begun the new age badly by taking up, like Paris,[1] a suspicious attitude to Greek.[2] 'At Cambridge,' wrote Sir Thomas More in 1519, 'which you were always wont to outshine, even those who do not learn Greek, are so far moved by a common zeal for their University that, to their credit be it told, they contribute to the salary of the Greek professor.'[3] And here begins to be seen what has become the predominant feature in Cambridge training and Cambridge thought—that steady interest in the fact, which in its higher flights becomes a burning passion for truth, leading men on to exploration in every field of study and life, and at its worst sinks to a heartless pedantry of accuracy. Cambridge has abundant illustrations of both extremes. But from this point onward one can point to this characteristic as salient in Cambridge life and the Cambridge mind. Oxford, it has been said, is the parent of great movements, and Cambridge of great men; but the great movements are not always forward, while the really great men of Cambridge have again and again lifted the thought of the nation to a new level—in poetry, in science, in religious experience.

VII

Erasmus was once for a time at Oxford, but it is with Cambridge and with Queens' College that his name is associated (1511–13). Here he lived and taught Greek; here, 'living like a snail in its shell', he prepared that edition of the Greek New Testament (1516),[4] which was so dynamic in European history. He did not like the Cambridge townspeople; but perhaps he must not be taken over-seriously on this point, as many who have lived fairly

1 P. Hume Brown, *George Buchanan*, p. 63.
2 An Oxford bookseller's ledger shows that in 1520 he sold 2383 books, some in English, most in Latin, one or two in Greek.
3 Erasmus says much the same; the monks at Oxford as elsewhere fought against Greek. The King had to issue warnings against the molestation of students of Greek at Oxford.
4 Erasmus, *Ep.* 115, 117 (Leyden), 225 (Allen).

contentedly with them have reserved the right to grumble at
them. Even the dons he perhaps found a trifle dull, though one
at least was a somewhat unusual man. 'We have a Doctor at the
University who has invented a Prophylactic of the Fifth Essence,
with which he promises to make old men young, and bring dead
men back to life; so that I may hope, if I swallow some of it, to
recover my own youth. If this prove true, I came to Cambridge
on a lucky day.'[1] Meanwhile he had to be content too often with
ale—on which reluctant contentment Thomas Fuller may be
quoted. Erasmus 'often complained of the *Colledge Ale, Cervisia
hujus loci mihi nullo modo placet,*[2] as raw, smal and windy; whereby
it appears,

'1. *Ale* in that age was the constant beverage of all *Colledges,*
before the Innovation of *beere* (the child of *Hops*) was brought
into England.

'2. *Queens Colledge Cervisia* was not *vis Cereris* but *Ceres
vitiata.* In my time (when I was a Member of that House)
scholars continued *Erasmus* his complaint whilest the *Brewers*
(having it seems prescription on their side for long time) little
amended it.

'The best was, Erasmus had his *Lagena* or *flagon* of Wine (recruited weekly from his friends at London) which he drank
sometimes singly by itselfe, and sometimes *incouraged* his *faint Ale*
with the mixture thereof.'

But England was not all small ale. 'To mention one attraction,'
writes Erasmus (*Ep.* 65) 'the English girls are divinely pretty.
Soft, pleasant, gentle, and charming as the Muses. They have
one custom which cannot be too much admired. When you
go anywhere on a visit, the girls all kiss you. They kiss you
when you arrive. They kiss you when you go away; and they
kiss you again when you return.' I do not know when this
interesting custom died out. Archaizing revivals are never very
successful.

1 Erasmus, *Ep.* 225 (Allen) Froude's translation.
2 Erasmus, *Ep.* 226 (Allen).

Years after he had left England, Erasmus in 1529 picked out three Colleges as foremost in the new learning—Queens', Christ's and St John's. What that new learning meant is put in a glowing passage by Milton: 'Then was the sacred BIBLE sought out of the dusty Corners where profane Falshood and Neglect had thrown it, the *Schools* opened, *Divine* and *Humane Learning* rak'd out of the *Embers* of *forgotten Tongues*, the *Princes* and *Cities* trooping apace to the new-erected *Banner of Salvation*; the *Martyrs* with the unresistible *might* of *Weakness*, shaking the *Powers* of *Darkness*, and scorning the *fiery Rage* of the old *red Dragon*.' Translated into Cambridge prose style, we find evidence for all this in new Colleges at Cambridge, new study of Greek and of the Greek Testament, and the Cambridge martyrs. Bilney, for instance, 'little Bilney', 'the blessed Saint Bilney', Latimer's friend and inspirer,[1] says he never saw the name of Jesus till he came on it in Erasmus' Greek Testament; and in the end he was martyred for it.

VIII

But first the new Colleges.

The Lady Margaret Beaufort, the mother of Henry VII, founded two of the new Colleges—Christ's and St John's; or rather she planned the foundation of St John's upon what remained of the Hospital of St John; but she died and left it to Bishop John Fisher to do. At the Quatercentenary of St John's Mr Justice Fletcher Moulton expressed himself as glad that he had not had to pronounce in his official capacity upon her will—or there would have been no College. But Fisher saw it through, and in 1511 the College was founded. It suffered in Henry VIII's reign, Fuller says, from 'a generation of proling, progging, projecting Promoters (such vermin like *Pharaohs Frogs* will sometimes creep even to *Kings Bedchambers*)'; but it throve. Trinity followed in 1546, by a fusion of old halls and houses and new endowment.

1 See Latimer's *Sermons*, no. 17, p. 334. He was martyred in 1529.

In the meantime Cambridge had given the nation the Reformation leaders. The stimulus of Erasmus' Greek Testament was supported by that of Luther's German writings. The books of Luther were indeed publicly burnt by the University authorities in 1521, on the order of Cardinal Wolsey. But proscription by authority does not always rob a book of readers. *Prohibiti sermones ideoque plures*, said Tacitus, and, if he did not mean Luther's sermons, it was none the less true of them. Somewhere between the Bull Hotel and King's College stood an inn, long gone (1823), the 'White Hart'. It could be approached from behind by a 'detestable and filthy' alley, called Plute's Lane, and by this path men made their way to it to study Luther, till the place got the nickname of 'Germany'. Many of the men in later years were burnt for the faith they first found there. Bilney was the centre of the group. Miles Coverdale and Frith, Tyndale's assistant, and perhaps Tyndale, were of it; Tyndale, whose translation gave to the Authorized Version itself the beauty that three hundred years and the 'tragic failure' (as *The Times* called it after fifty years) of the Revised Version have only heightened, was at Cambridge in those days and may very well have first conceived of his great work in the secret room of the 'White Hart'. Aldis Wright doubted whether Tyndale could have attended lectures of Erasmus. It would seem that, among the followers of Wiclif, the educated and well-to-do recanted when it came to the stake and the fire; now Cambridge men, though some apostatized, were conspicuous for facing martyrdom and going through with it; and the impress on England was indelible. As Latimer, master to the end of the vigorous and racy English that keeps his sermons alive, said to Ridley, a candle was lighted which never was put out. And both of them, and Cranmer too, were Cambridge men. The Castle Hill, in those days, got the nickname of Heretics' Hill from the frequency with which Bilney and Latimer were seen walking about it. Two sentences may come in here from Bishop Nix of Norwich—'accombered with suche as kepith and redeth these Arronious bokes in engleshe and beleve and gif credence to the same and teacheth other that they shuld so doo'—'Ther is', he says, 'a collage in Cambridge called gunwell haule of the foundacion of a Bishoppe of Norwiche. I here of no clerke that hath come aught lately of that collage but saverith of the friainge panne thoughe he speke never so holely.'[1]

In Mary's reign the University declined. Cambridge was already predominantly Protestant; so its statutes were overhauled, and its teachers and students fled. Gardiner was severe in his treatment of St John's and Trinity. Ascham says, and Caius confirms it, that Cambridge reached its lowest under the Catholic regime. Between 1555 and 1559 only 179 men proceeded to the B.A. degree.[2] From the reconciliation with Rome to Mary's death no Oxford or Cambridge College bought any but service books.[3] Learning does not go comfortably with reaction, as Cambridge learnt again in the eighteenth century. John Caius, however, came back and refounded Gonville Hall—a Papist physician and a personality. The deaf, the dumb, the deformed and the lame, he debarred from scholarships in his College—and with them the Welshman. Somehow Cambridge has never had many Welshmen.

Bishop Fisher watched over his new foundation with the utmost care for some twenty years. A Fellow in those days, we learn, received as 'commons' (a grant toward the cost of his food) an allowance of one shilling a day (a scholar must do with sevenpence), but also a stipend of one mark (13s. 4d.) per annum, with certain other emoluments for livery, barber and washerman. The last Fellow of St John's to receive special allowances for 'livery' and for 'brawn' died a few years ago.

It was not long after its foundation that the College fell into very desperate difficulties. The immense influx into Europe of precious metals from Mexico and Peru sent up the prices of every

1 A. W. Pollard, *Records of the English Bible*, no. xx, p. 161.
2 W. H. Woodward, *Camb. Eng. Lit.* iii, p. 421. On the other hand, in the single year 1584 the B.A.'s were more than 200.
3 Thorold Rogers, *Hist. of Agriculture and Prices*, iv, p. 602.

commodity, changed the values of land, and set wool-growing in the ascendant; and as in the nineteenth century, when the Western States and Manitoba plunged English farming into new difficulties, the Colleges suffered—*misera hac rerum caritate, fame et frigore enecti jacemus*; and how (the question was addressed to Queen Mary) could some live on sevenpence a week and others on threepence? 'We shall be done for', the Archbishop of York was told, '*actum plane erit de nobis et studiis nostris*, through this intolerable rise of prices' (*hanc intollerabilem charitatem rerum*—a nobler phrase than 'H.C.L.' but as sad). But somehow the College survived, finding, as many Colleges have done in older days and more modern times, 'pious benefactors'.

From time to time St John's, like other Colleges, was faced with other problems than national and international. Anxious work as it was to face Mexican gold, changes of religion and foreign and civil wars, there was the administration of estates; and Sir Henry Howard, in his history of College finance, has to spend time and space on the varieties of lease and fine, and the precarious return they might yield the College. Sometimes College officials too seem to have lacked sense (financial sense and other kinds of sense), certainly energy, and now and then the higher elements of honesty. Gwyn, for instance, Master from 1612 to 1633, 'sits down and reposes himself amongst his seniors'; and Thomas Baker, the historian, a century later offers the story 'as a useful precaution to posterity not to venture too much upon irregular things by presuming too much upon impunity'.

With Elizabeth better times generally came for Cambridge— new life and a larger contribution to the nation. She visited the place herself in 1564, riding on her palfrey into the hall of St John's—a procedure no longer used on royal visits. She gave the University new statutes which lasted till 1849—not an unmixed boon, for as one says who was long associated with reform movements in the nineteenth century and was himself Head of a House, they transformed the ancient democracy into an oligarchic government—both within and without the College walls.[1] And the Heads, says a contemporary critic, 'keepe Benefices and be non-residentes. While they are clothed in scarlet [as Doctors, no doubt], their flocks perish for cold; and while they fare deliciouslie, ther people are faint with a most miserable hunger.' But the change was made, and it lasted. Heads of Houses are great and august figures, but they do not comprise the whole of College life, especially if they are non-resident. 'When once a man has his rump in the seat of a head,' said Adam Sedgwick the elder (in the mid-nineteenth century), 'his whole moral nature becomes inverted.' (Perhaps he was a shade blunter.)

IX

In a letter of Gabriel Harvey's written to the poet Spenser in 1579–80, we have in rather fanciful language a curiously vivid picture of the life and interests of the place.

' *Tully* and *Demosthenes* nothing so much studied as they were wont; *Livy* and *Sallust* perhaps more, rather than less; *Lucian* never so much; *Aristotle* much named but little read; *Xenophon* and *Plato* reckoned amongst discoursers and conceited superficial fellows; much verbal and sophistical jangling; little subtle and effectual disputing. *Machiavel* a great man; *Castilio*, of no small repute; *Petrarch* and *Boccace* in every man's mouth;...the *French* and *Italian* highly regarded; the *Latin* and *Greek* but lightly... new *books*, new fashions, new laws, new officers, and some after new elements, some after new heavens and hells too. *Turkish* affairs familiarly known; castles built in the air; much ado and little help; in no age so little so much made of; every one highly in his own favour....The Gospel taught, not learnt; Charity cold; nothing good but by imputation; the Ceremonial Law in word abrogated; the Judicial in effect disannull'd, the Moral abandon'd; *the Light, the Light,* in every man's lips, but mark their eyes, and you will say they are rather like owls than eagles....Every day spawns new opinions; heresy in divinity, in philosophy, in

1 John Peile, *Christ's College*, p. 79.

humanity, in manners grounded upon hearsay; doctors con-
temn'd; the *devil* not so hated as the *pope*; many invectives, but
no amendment. No more ado about caps and surplices; Mr
Cartwright quite forgotten.'

No one expects a satirist to be pedantic in his loyalty to history,
but there is plenty of history in this letter. Spenser had been at
Pembroke College from 1569 to 1576, and some of the interests
which Harvey thus runs over were no novelties. For Turkish
affairs, the battle of Lepanto had been fought in 1571—as significant a victory over barbarism as fleet ever won. The Bartholomew massacre took place on 24 August 1572, which, with
the Pope's triumphal medal for it, might give fervid natures
excuse for hating him worse than an invisible fiend. Mr Cartwright's stormy career as Lady Margaret professor had begun and
ended in Spenser's College days; but surplices were not quite
done with. 'The ghost of a linen decency haunts us yet', as Milton
wrote. In 1584 three hundred Fellows and scholars of St John's
elected to go to Chapel without surplices, and made a fresh stir.
So much for outer events. Where were men's personal interests?
The University exacted Greek and Latin; for the Classics were
valued in those days. The crescendo of abuse on the curate, quoted
in Latimer's sermon, betrays it: 'Our curate is naught; an ass-
head; a dodipole; a lack-Latin.' Fisher's statutes for St John's required a composition in Latin verse and one in Greek verse every
week from each scholar; and I rejoice to think that I still did them,
one at least of one or other sort every week, and there are few
better disciplines, as Melanchthon and George Buchanan, and
probably William Cowper, would agree. But Spenser, like
Wordsworth two centuries later, strayed to French and Italian
poets, prescribed neither by statutes nor by Heads, and did so to
the lasting gain of English poetry. For Harvey failed to induce
Spenser to write for long in English hexameters. The poet Nash
has left a picture of Harvey that supplements his own in the letter
—'the carrying up of his gown, his nice gait in his pantoffles, the
affected accent of his speech'.

Cambridge had men of other interests too, who probably appealed little to Harvey, or not at all—Bacon of Trinity—Gilbert, Senior Bursar of St John's (1569), whom Galileo praised as 'great to a degree that might be envied', who wrote *de Magnete*, and 'is thus acclaimed as the originator, in both its branches, of the vast modern electric development, which on the technical side has now dominated all engineering practice, and on the theoretical side lies at the very foundation of Natural Philosophy'[1]—and a more famous Harvey, of Caius, who discovered, according to Charles Lamb, that the blood is red.

The seventeenth century is full of great men and great deeds that thrill us yet, and Cambridge and her sons bore their part with the best. Cambridge contributed some sixty graduates to Massachusetts as against twenty Oxford men[2], a fact that led to the re-naming of the town where Harvard College was to be. Oliver Cromwell was at Sidney Sussex College, and was M.P. for the borough.[3] The Colleges sent their plate to King Charles, and had Parliamentary troops billeted upon them, which intelligibly they did not like.[4] The town was the key to East Anglia, and Cromwell held it. The great poets of England and some smaller ones, as in other centuries, were sons of Cambridge—Milton (who wrote his Ode on the Nativity during his Cambridge days) and Dryden (who deserted us 'in his riper age'), George Herbert and others. But for the present we will let the legions thunder past—probably on their way to Oxford and other important places, to make English history—and we will ourselves turn to people so trivial as the undergraduates, the majority after all in any well-conducted University.

1 Sir Joseph Larmor.   2 Oviatt, *The Beginnings of Yale*, p. 54.
3 See Atkinson and Clark, p. 102.
4 Tatham, *The Puritans in Power*, ch. 4, p. 104; St John's alas! sent 2065¼ oz. of silver which got through; the Magdalene and Trinity Hall contributions were intercepted.

X

The British Museum keeps some hundreds of letters written by members of a Norfolk family of this century, whose name was Gawdy. Mr Venn has selected and printed a number of these letters which describe life at Caius at the period—the actual letters written by his undergraduate sons to Framlingham Gawdy, Esquire, of West Harling. Six of his sons and a nephew were at the College, and none of them wrote for posterity, though the nephew has a magnificent style which may have impressed his parishioners in later days, unless he grew out of it. The others write quite simply—often for money in so many words. 'There are many', writes William about 1632, 'in our Colledge who doo thinke that I am so miserable that I will not part withe my money, and oftentimes doo deride mee for it; which faulte (you knowe) lies not in my power to mend unless I had wherwithal to shew myself more free and liberall. It is not the covetousnesse of my minde which makes me thus, but only the want and scarsity of money. Every one doo expecte of mee, being a fellowe commoner, that I should live after the fashion of a gentleman, whiche by no means in the world I can accomplishe without the helpe of money. I knowe it is your desire that I should live conformable to my callinge'; and the inevitable request follows. To another letter he appends a postscript: 'When you sende me a letter backe againe you should doe very well to put an angel or halfe a piece into it.' Bunyan says that Christiana tipped the porter at the Palace Beautiful with an angel, and he made her a low obeisance. Bassingbourne Gawdy, a younger brother, makes 'no question but that I shall live very well upon 60 li. per annum'.

Clothes occupy their minds—clothes sometimes sent from home, sometimes provided by the tutor. William wants a new hat 'for my ole one beginnes to growe unfitting for a gentleman to weare'; 'I pray let it be new shagged thoughe it bee somewhat the thinner and (if it be possible) let it be made lesse in the heade, and let the brimmes be cut somewhat narrower as the fashion is; and I pray let mee have a silver girdle of the best sort...and I will pay you for it againe' (13 Nov. 1631). In another letter (undated) the hat is to have 'a new silver hatband of the best fashion'. Bass. (as he signs himself) is more moderate in hats—'I heard by Ro. Green that you had a hatte which was too little four you, which if you please to give it me I will be a very good husband in wearing it, for I have but one, and I wear that every day.' But Bass. has his own extravagances: 'Sir you write to me to forbear silver buttons, but bothe my Tutor and Mr Anderson did perswade me to it; it did cost but 20s the more: if you think it too much I will abate it in my allowance.' Cousin Antony writes for a 'shute', since 'I confess it is the time now when nature doeth cloeth all hir creatures: the earth with grasse, as the cloeth, and with diversitye of flowers as it were the triming or setting out of the garment', to say nothing of 'yor own yarde', and then 'gowe we a little higher and behowld the birdes of the aier'. William is 'altogether destitute of a weapon', 1 May 1632, and daily expects the arrival of Mr Rawlins 'with my sword by his side'. His Bible has been stolen from his rooms, and he would like another sent; 'let Rawlins binde it up in paper and binde two pieces of pastbord over it, and it can take noe hurt'. 'I would entreat that my cosen Doll may make us a great Cake or twoe, and withall a cheese or twoe will doe very well to amend our poore lenten commons.'

Forgotten social customs occur in the letters. William has to be 'senior brother in the Commencement house this yeare, which is a place of very great credite, but withall very chargeable, for I should have given the proctours each of them a sattin doublet, and should have invited all the doctors and chiefe men in the towne to supper'. Charles is 'deeply ingaged to a prockter in Cambridge a dear friende of myne to doe him so much favour as to give him a Bucke this commensment'. A fellow-commoner has a sizar to wait on him. Bass. wants napkins to use in hall, and 'my spare hawke'; and instructions are given about horses to meet them as they come home; or news is sent of smallpox 'reife in the towne' or many dying every week 'of agues and other diseases'. Only one of the six brothers took a degree; fashion was then not exacting about it.

XI

Here is another glimpse at Cambridge, twenty years later, 1655, through the eyes of a critic—George Fox:[1]

'And after this I passt to Cambridge y^t eveninge & when I came Into ye tounde ye schollors was uppe hearinge of mee: & was exceedinge rude: but I kept on my horse backe & ridd through y^m in ye Lords power: oh saide they he shines he glisters:[2] but they unhorst Capt Amor Stodart before hee coulde gett to ye Inn: & when we was in an Inn they was exceedinge rude in ye Inn & in ye Courtes & in ye streetes.

'The miners & colliers & cart men could never be ruder: & there Jo: Crooke met us att ye Inn.

'And the people of ye house askt mee what I would have for supper as is ye usuall way of Inns: supper saide I: were it not y^t ye Lords power was over these rude schollors: lookt as if they woulde make a supper of us: & plucke us to peices: for they knew I was soe against there trade: which they were there as Apprentices to learne ye trade of preachinge y^t they raged as bad as ever Dianas Craftsmen did against Paul.'

In 1660 King Charles II came back,[3] and in two years the Act of Uniformity made, as Pepys foresaw, 'mad work among the

1 Two years before, two Quakeresses had been stripped naked to the waist and flogged at the Market Cross, their bodies being slashed and torn exceedingly: W. C. Braithwaite, *Beginnings of Quakerism*, p. 295. It was more usually the punishment of loose women.

2 Anyone who knows the Swarthmore portrait of George Fox will see that they meant his eyes.

3 It is perhaps relevant to mention that Charles II invented the Newmarket race-meeting (first parent of all such meetings in Anglo-Saxon lands)—of which regular notice used to be given to undergraduates of my College by the dean's prohibition of our attending the races.

Presbyterian ministers'. Cambridge had suffered expulsions under Mary, Elizabeth and the Parliament; and now once more, but, as Mr Godley says of Oxford,[1] it was the work of the Government, not of the University. Other Acts of a vindictive character followed to harry dissent out of existence. One of them receives curious illustration in a Cambridge story of those days.[2] The Conventicle Act (1670) provided that if two witnesses swore before a Justice of the Peace to having seen any person, of the age of sixteen or upward, at a nonconformist meeting for worship—five persons to constitute a meeting—the Justice might there and then fine that person, without further ado, five shillings, or, in case of a second offence, ten. Such proceedings must be taken within three months of the offence. There was also a provision that one-third of the fine should be paid to the informers.

Now there was in Cambridge one Stephen Perry, a brazier by trade, and by principle a maintainer of the Royal House and the Church of England. It was not every one whose conscience was so stirred, but Stephen Perry flung himself with zeal and energy into the business of making the Conventicle Act a reality. We need not impute motives.[3] But when he went to Sir Thomas Slater, Fellow of Trinity and Justice of the Peace, to lay information about a conventicle of fifteen persons at Toft, Slater 'said he was not at leisure. The next day I went to him, then alsoe he made answer that he was busie'. And so it went on till the three months were expired, and Stephen found himself threatened at law—perhaps for malicious prosecution or defamation or law knows what. Stephen saw he must look higher, to 'be back'd out from above'.

So he went to Dr Turner, the Master of St John's, with a statement of the case to be presented to the King or the Duke of York.

1 A. D. Godley, *Oxford in the 18th Century*, p. 44.

2 This story was disinterred from the St John's College records by Sir Robert Scott, and printed in *The Eagle*, May, 1908.

3 Perry is otherwise notorious, being the subject of a tract of 1675, called *Newes from Cambridge*.

He also 'could not forbear bragging among the boys that he had acquainted his Majesty with all his matters'. Before very long he received a letter, in the following tenour:

CHARLES R.

WEE have received your letter from the hands of our Secretary wherein we are informed of your complaints against Sir Thomas Slater, Justice of our Peace, how he hath not proceeded according to the order prescribed in our late Act, ratifyed in our late Session of Parliament. Wee do will and require you in our name forthwith to acquaint the said Sir Thomas Slater to be more vigorous in his proceedings, or he shall appeare before our Council Board to answer those things objected against him. We do furthermore authorize you to goe on in that part of a loyal subject as you have begun and in our name to show these our letters patents to our Maior of Cambridge, that he may uindicate you with his authority in your office, delivered in the presence of our Chief Secretary

ARLINGTON

Given at our Court of Whitehall February 17 in the year of our Lord 1670, in the three and twentieth yeare of our reign.

Addressed: to our Trusty and wellbeloved Stephen Perry, Brasier, Cambridge.

A seal was appended; so the thing was above suspicion.

The Mayor was duly impressed; but not the Master of St John's, when Perry showed it to him 'with a great deal of joy'. For Masters of Colleges are not always so guileless as is supposed. That seal—it was odd that a Royal letter should be sealed with the back of a five-shilling-piece. (Charles II was notoriously short of money, for one thing—a modern reflects.) 'With much adoe I persuaded Mr Maior and our Informer that they were both gull'd.' But Mayors of Cambridge are solemn men—not to be played with; had not an undergraduate stood for three hours with his ear nailed to the pillory in 1569 for speaking 'evyll and fowle words' to the Mayor?[1] So the Mayor went to the Vice-Chancellor, and so did the Master. A letter was written to Lord Arlington, enclosing the one with his signature, and an apology from Mr Lewis Maidwell of St John's, stating that he had acted 'not out of any ill intention, but to make sport with the saide Stephen Perry'. And as Lewis Maidwell, vouched for as 'one of excellent facultye', took his B.A. degree a year later, it looks as if the Master's view prevailed. One can hardly imagine King Charles perturbed about the affair.

The undergraduate hoax is always with us—did not a certain Mayor of Cambridge entertain the Sultan of Zanzibar once, though another Sultan of Zanzibar of at least equal authenticity stayed in London that day? Was there not in 1919-20 positively a 'Bolshevik army' (of undergraduates) with its headquarters in Pembroke College (of all places) sworn to 'debag' the Navy students—an allegation taken so seriously that 'the Navy' was 'gated' to avoid conflicts? But what a picture the episode gives us—the harried dissenters—the decent Justice who despised Act and informer—the bright lad—the acute Master (afterwards one of the Seven Bishops whom James II sent to the Tower)—and the squalour of Restoration ways of restoring true religion!

XII

But now a glance at things more serious. Gilbert and Harvey we have noted as explorers of Truth of the true Cambridge breed. We must not forget Milton, who gave up the idea of a Christ's Fellowship to keep freedom of conscience, and lived and died a pioneer in the realm of ideas and in the realm of beauty. Newton, too, illustrates the passion for Truth that our University wakes in her best sons. They are not always recognized in their lifetimes;

1 Atkinson and Clark, p. 38.

we cannot suppose that Christ's in Charles II's reign emphasized
its connexion with Milton, but in Edward VII's the College dined
in splendour to show its admiration for its poet, beside com-
memorating him in other ways. The spirit, however, of resolute
inquiry recurs again·and again in the records of Cambridge men,
and again and again it is crowned with discovery—new regions
of thought opened up to men, new visions set before them. *Multi
pertransibunt*, quoted Bacon, one of this type himself, *et augebitur
Scientia.*

Despite Lewis Maidwell and his kind, in spite of Newton, and
even in spite of Bentley, dullness came over Cambridge with the
Restoration, and grew more intense and colossal as George followed George. Gray was at Cambridge, but it was not a very
interesting Cambridge. Whether Zachary Brooke shall become
Lady Margaret Professor—or did—is not a theme to make heart
beat; he is long dead, *et opera illius sequuntur illum*, as happens to
many a professor even in more conscientious times. The dons
neglected their duties, and their pupils did not fall short of so
engaging an example. Cowper, writing of Cambridge, which he
used to visit from Huntingdon, excepted his brother's College,
Corpus, as one 'in which Order yet is sacred', and then he altered
is to *was*.[1] He speaks of 'drinkers, gamesters, fornicators, lewd
talkers, and profane jesters—men, in short, of no principles either
religious or moral—and such we know are the majority of those
sent out by our Universities'. One hesitates to accept so sweeping
an estimate—was not William Unwin a Cambridge man?—but
no one gives the place in the eighteenth century a very good
name. Bentley fought the Fellows of Trinity at the beginning
of the century—a great figure in scholarship; but Richard Watson,
Bishop of Llandaff, non-resident bishop and professor at once,
seems a more typical figure at the end. Gunning's *Reminiscences*
do not lead us to fresh doubts of Cowper's lament. He draws the
portraits of commonplace men, with vulgar instincts and coarse
habits, little touched by reflexion or ideal. But Gunning perhaps

[1] Letter to William Unwin, 20 Nov. 1784.

was not a natural recipient of the confidences of the spiritual or intellectual type.

William Wordsworth came to St John's in 1787, and within twenty years wrote his impressions of Cambridge, vivid and familiar. We know his dons—'old men, unscoured, grotesque of character'. They survive in cartoons of a later generation, drawn horribly to the life. He found the system of education dull; and the compulsory chapels, not abolished till after the Peace of 1919, though the rule was relaxed, he abhorred. He was chiefly indebted to Cambridge for 'the advantages to be derived from the neglect of his teachers'.[1] He let a Fellowship slide, in order not to be overdone with Mathematics, as his sister confessed. What he did, he tells us in *The Prelude*:

> We sauntered, played, or rioted; we talked
> Unprofitable talk at morning hours,
> Drifted about along the streets and walks,
> Read lazily in trivial books, went forth
> To gallop through the country in blind zeal
> Of senseless horsemanship, or on the breast
> Of Cam sailed boisterously, and let the stars
> Come forth, perhaps without one quiet thought.

The last line is the criticism. He wore powdered hair and silk stockings—not unsupported by Dorothy, one guesses, who admired the 'smart powdered heads' of the students as she passed through. But he read other than trivial books. He studied Italian with Isola, grandfather of Charles Lamb's adopted daughter, and

> Beside the pleasant Mill of Trumpington
> I laughed with Chaucer in the hawthorn shade.

Spenser, too, he studied:

> Sweet Spenser moving through his clouded heaven—
> With the moon's beauty and the moon's soft pace;
> I called him Brother, Englishman and Friend.

[1] Leslie Stephen.

Milton he honoured, as we know, by 'pouring libations' in his room at Christ's, and, we may guess, in other ways. Coleridge, who came up a little later, had still more extended interests. The signatures of both are to be seen in the University register, and Coleridge's autograph copy of the Greek Ode, with which he won Sir William Browne's gold medal in 1792—in great, sprawling, lazy Greek characters. Cambridge in those days, it may be of interest to note, had a population of 9063, to whom the University added 805 more (1794).[1]

But in spite of the energetic and reforming Master, Dr Powell (1765 to 1775), the nineteenth century saw St John's College languishing for thirty years under a clerical bursar, who had a positive gift for mismanagement. Thus the familiar 'New Court' of St John's (built during his reign, but now not supremely admired either by visitors, or architects, or even the tenants in its rooms) cost £77,000 odd to build, and another £40,000 odd to pay for it. So Sir Henry Howard calculates from the tangles and contradictions of lax methods. Later again in the nineteenth century, the Gilbert Scott chapel cost £78,000 to build and £20,000 in interest charges.

The nineteenth century is the period of the Nationalization of our old Universities—at first a process tardy, cautious and reluctant, while since 1882 a good deal has been done, as we shall see in another chapter, by influences not quite reckoned upon. Even in Tennyson's day—1828 and onwards—Cambridge was dull and backward, if beautiful. His own group was a very unusual one at any time, but, for the University at large, he wrote in 1830:

> Therefore your Halls, your ancient Colleges,
> Your portals statued with old kings and queens,
> Your gardens, myriad-volumed libraries,
> Wax-lighted chapels, and rich carven screens,
> Your doctors and your proctors and your deans,
> Shall not avail you when the Day-beam sports
> New-risen o'er awaken'd Albion. No!

1 Gunning's *Reminiscences*, i, p. 318.

Nor yet your solemn organ-pipes that blow
Melodious thunders through your vacant courts
At noon and eve, because your manner sorts
Not with this age, wherefrom ye stand apart,
Because the lips of little children preach
Against you, you that do profess to teach
And teach us nothing, feeding not the heart.

But in conclusion to this chapter of our retrospect, let us listen to Carlyle. 'One benefit', he wrote, 'not to be dissevered from the most obsolete University still frequented by young ingenuous living souls, is that of manifold collision and communication with the said young souls. In this point, as the learned Huber has insisted, the two English Universities...far excel all other.' And of the two, he says, Sterling chose Cambridge as 'decidedly the more catholic (not Roman catholic, but Human catholic)', and there he caught 'the humour and creed of College Radicalism'—'a young ardent soul looking with hope and joy into a world which was infinitely beautiful to him, though overhung with falsities and foul cobwebs as world never was before; overloaded, over-clouded, to the zenith and the nadir of it by incredible uncredited traditions, solemnly sordid hypocrisies, and beggarly deliriums old and new; which latter class of objects it was clearly the part of every noble heart to expend all its lightnings and energies in burning up without delay, and sweeping into their native Chaos out of such a Cosmos as this'.

That is not quite undergraduate language; yet if we admit Pendennis' Oxbridge and Christopher Wordsworth's Trinity as evidence to reduce its temperature, Carlyle is right; and they think so still:

Ἡμεῖς τοι πατέρων μέγ' ἀμείνονες εὐχόμεθ' εἶναι.

And why not? Cambridge is reformed, and reformed again; it is married and conscientious and scientific, steeped in 'research'; and still they think like Sterling. Brave lads! It is the Cambridge spirit after all. In the last chapter readers will find more about the undergraduate, some of it from his own hand.

Chapter II

CLASSICAL

I

When I first knew St John's, there were six Classical men on the staff, of whom, in accordance with old tradition, three had come from Shrewsbury School. But reformers cut the tie that bound the School to the College, and some of the distinction that marked it passed away when Benjamin Hall Kennedy ceased to be its tremendous headmaster, a great personality and famous for his scholars as well. The training had been in what we more narrowly called scholarship, a precise grip of language, invaluable if learning is to be maintained, a necessary foundation for all real advance in Classical studies, but not in itself everything. It did not please Henry Jackson. A bust and a portrait of Kennedy are in St John's; the bust apparently more successful than the portrait—the painter, according to Graves, had shut Kennedy's mouth tighter than the living man had ever been able to keep it. It is two long generations since Kennedy's headmastership, and a modern day misses in his work what it looks for. What Kennedy would say about our modern scholarship, if he could come back, I dare not guess. 'Boy!' he would roar across the classroom, W. F. Smith told me; and he was very definite as to who was and who was not a scholar. 'Where did you get that rendering?' he demanded of a boy construing Horace. 'From my father's edition', said the young Macleane. 'Poor boy!' the headmaster was heard to murmur, 'his father is not a scholar.' Heitland was the third of the three Salopians on my list. Kennedy was Professor of Greek for a year or two more after my first coming to Cambridge; I never saw him, but I learnt that he was one of the examiners for the Porson Prize and saw my first year work.

Heitland was my tutor—William Emerton Heitland, to give
him his full name—a 'character' (if one may use that abused
word), like nobody else. 'He's an oddity', said his old mother to
me; she ought to have known, for they were very like in features,
and in ways too (I think); and she added, 'but men like him.'
She was right in both particulars. Our relations began with storm.
In the summer of 1888 a Bristol friend, a member of Clare and
afterwards professor at Bristol University, was going to Cambridge and offered to see Heitland about the rooms I might have
that October. George Hare Leonard was one of the most delightful men I have known, whichever way you took him. This is
what followed—a letter from Heitland about his visitor—'I had
to get rid of him in a hurry' (you may be sure he did) 'and I trust
I gave no offence' (I think Leonard was more amused than
offended; that sort of thing happened). 'But I write now to say
that such proceeding does not *save me trouble* (as he seemed to
think) but *gives me trouble*. Will you in future communicate *with
me*. It is always best not to try indirect means till direct ones fail.
...I am not well, and this sudden invasion did me no good, I
assure you.' Two days later (apparently after a letter from me)
he returned to the charge: 'Please understand that your claim
comes in a certain order, after some, before others. You cannot
write and order such and such a set....Meanwhile, be sure that
I shall not forget the claims of those who give little or no trouble.'
But he would always be glad to see my Father, 'not a third party';
and see him he did; and when October came, the storm had blown
over. But he was an alarming correspondent for a schoolboy.
Heitland was always apt to be tragic. 'No treatment is too bad
for a tutor', he would say. One of his pupils told me he always
began an interview by expressing the hope that Heitland 'was
better'.

Now pass over ten years, and here is another missive, sent to me
in Canada. The note is different. I had written him about his
article on the hephthemimeral pause in the Latin hexameter.
I won't explain it here, but it was a signal study. 'However,' he

wrote, 'χαιρέτω. I am full up with history work these 14 or 15 months past' (those who read his Roman History will believe it). 'Keep your pecker up', he went on; 'soon *contigerit Geticis melior fortuna colonis, tuque Tomitanae pars bona plebis eris.* I hope to be with my Mother at Salop 6 weeks in Aug.–Sept. *Hic pessimi exempli, ut mos est, omnia. Felix qui non adsis aut haec φορτικώτατα videas. Scilicet libros excutis, mosquitos interficis—immo conaris inter- ficere, uxori filiolae operam das, νέα γὰρ νηδύς...elegantiae trans- marinae cottidie aliquid hauris. Credo te brevi germanum πολίτην fore. Sed instat tabellarius, et tu et Terentia tua bene valeatis. Dabam ante Aul a d iv kal Aug.*' I don't translate and I don't add punctua- tion—Salopians had a fancy for discarding it. But there is a dif- ferent tone in the two periods of correspondence. Ten years had intervened, and the reader of the later communication does not need to be told how relations had developed. I think everybody who knew Heitland will feel that this bilingual post-card carries a great deal of the man—friendship, humour, irritation, industry, geniality, and once more the tragic touch; things, especially in College, were apt to be *pessimi exempli.* He was periodically immensely vext at things and people in College, and, when he was vext, people knew it; but a kindliness co-existed with his irritability. For instance, in those days there was no 'College nurse'—there were hardly any nurses at all—and my friend Dicky Benthall was very ill, really dangerously ill; and Heitland sat up with him three consecutive nights. What happened to pupils who called on him and crossed him on the fourth afternoon, no one told me. They probably had their heads bitten off, and forgave him when they heard about Benthall. When Heitland had his big illness in College in 1893, one of the scholars met me. How was old Billy? he wanted to know; and suggested that, if he was not really mending and quick about it, we should sacrifice one of the other tutors to the infernal gods as a substitute. But his medical man took things seriously, and Heitland after a little had three nurses, and guided by Professor Bradbury—and no doubt helped by his own constitution—they balked the infernal gods, who didn't get any of our tutors for many years. I borrow the phrase, you see, and speak paganly. Let us get back to Heitland.

He was, so to put it, at once a terror and a delight; and you never quite knew which he would be. He would see his pupils daily between 5.30 and 7 p.m. That was written up on his door; his handwriting was characteristic, carefully formed and intended to be legible, as it was; and how well I remember a scene at that door. I caught it for coming too soon—no doubt about that; then we each got out his watch, and (if I remember) it was approximately 5.27 p.m.; so my delinquency was overlooked, and relations resumed. Only you must not move your chair; he sat square at his desk; your chair was at exactly the right angle to him and his desk, and it was perilous to shift it an inch—there would be 'a cry of pain', some one said, and the comment was instantly recognized as true. But once these difficulties of hour and angle were surmounted, provided no fresh ones occurred, all would be well and could even be delightful. For he stood by his pupils, when he was clear that they were right and straight, whether clever or not. Dicky Benthall again—Dicky was a great tennis player, and going across the court one morning in tennis clothes he was caught by the Senior Dean; such garb was forbidden in morning hours. But how was Dicky to reach the paddock except by crossing the court? I don't know how Cox parried that, if he did. 'I see', said Dicky in his matter-of-fact way, 'that you don't mean to answer me.' The Dean exploded and there was trouble. Dicky went at once to his tutor. 'No,' said Heitland, 'you shouldn't have said that; you will have to apologize....' Dicky murmured something...'*Of course* make him answer you', said the tutor. Cox should never have been Dean; he didn't do as Dean, and his colleague was beyond words worse. The wicked Heitland had a way of making Cox into two syllables with the aid of Aristophanes—βρεκεκεκὲξ κοὰξ κοάξ. I have to own I did not like Cox when I was young and he was Dean; but years together at the High Table changed all that.

Instead of a gloomy and unsympathetic would-be authority I
found a most kindly, courteous and scholarly old gentleman, and
grew fond of him. Angle means a good deal in friendship.
  Heitland had heaps of angles. Some innocent British child was
once asked what a Quaker was; 'two crotchets', he replied.
I can't guess how many crotchets Heitland had—and much beside
crotchets. I have referred to his Roman History, a very big bit
of work, in which, according to a Cambridge scholar of another
College, he 'beat Mommsen on Mommsen's own ground'.
I would hardly say so much; I grew up on Mommsen, and
Mommsen's History is a much more brilliant book than Heitland's, in which I have always somehow felt myself halted—never
quite getting there. He seems to stop before all is said—a Cambridge habit of mind, perhaps. Though he was far from being a
typical Cambridge man, the spirit of the place had helped to shape
him, as it does with all of us. Accept or rebel, you don't get away
from your environment; you cannot be born about 1847 as he
was and belong to another age; a Cambridge man cannot by any
manner of conversion become anything else. His other big book
I found more contributive. *Agricola* is a most full and learned
inquiry into the conditions of agricultural labour in antiquity—
its supply, failure, consequences and so forth. It was based on the
widest reading of the Classics, done with a German thoroughness,
and something better which is not very common in learned works
imported from Germany. The book was new, a fresh inquiry
made by a really alert mind, a man who knew quite well what he
was doing and was equal to it. It came out at a bad time, and the
publisher put a tremendous price on it. As Sir Joshua Reynolds
said, you can't be sure how a book will be taken, and in those days
publishers were apt to be gloomy about the prospects of books
and authors; 'it is nought, it is nought', saith the buyer. Heitland
said afterwards that he would gladly have made a considerable
contribution in cash to the cost of production to have secured the
sale of the book at a lower price.
  In my day he did no teaching; I never quite understood why,

either then or later. He was Tutor and Junior Bursar, in charge of men and buildings. I have some vague impression, which cannot now be verified, that he flung out of his lectureship, to make it possible for the College Council to appoint some one else to lecture—I think Tottenham, to whom they had engaged themselves somehow. Few of my contemporaries would say that the College teaching gained by losing Heitland's presence in Lecture Room VI.

Here is a document found among R. F. Scott's papers, never repeated, long forgotten—perhaps because effectual; certainly characteristic.

> I take leave to point out that the practice of throwing into the courts and grounds such articles as matches, paper, orange-peel, slices of lemon, and other scraps and refuse objects, is not one likely to improve the appearance of the College or to convey a good impression to our visitors. Also that the reason why such acts are not expressly forbidden by a College rule is that they are deemed unlikely to suggest themselves to men who have a character for decent conduct to maintain. Also that they are very hard to detect and are almost always perpetrated with impunity. Also that they are such as the weakest of mankind would be able to perform, if placed in a position to do so.
>
> I have therefore no doubt that the general opinion of members of the College will operate to prevent such acts in future as out of place and discreditable to our Society.
>
> W E HEITLAND
Junior Bursar.
>
> *St John's College,*
> *June* 13 1887.

Still he seemed really interested in fabric and buildings, and he loved a ladder. Lecturer or not he counted with his own Classical pupils. He now and then did a little composition with them. It was a drastic discipline; perhaps the work, he said, would have been better if you had spent *less* pains upon it. Perhaps it would have; but it is a Cambridge characteristic to trust supremely to industry and not everybody here could criticize it as Heitland did. Perhaps he was amenable to his own canon, and his own Roman History suffered from his spending too much pains upon it.

Of course, one cannot think of Heitland without recalling the History, the *Agricola* and notably his introduction to Haskins's edition of Lucan, which was far and away the more valuable half of that book. But any one who lived alongside of Heitland, nearer or further, for forty years thinks of much else before the books. The extraordinary freakish humour, the genial fun, the savage fun, the quip, the verse, the incalculable angle, made him always interesting; you were always watching. I never forgot the shock, when, one evening shortly after my return from Canada, I called at his new house and he suddenly blazed out that he had left College to get away from people. The rebuff made it clear there would be no resumption of the old intimacy; it did not mean that all kindness ceased. Only one had to be careful. A later generation knew him chiefly at the College meeting—bobbing about the room with his hand at his ear, to hear each speaker in turn, with sudden interjections. He knew a great deal more about the College than most of us, and brought odd memories to bear in odd ways. Sometimes he addressed us—his hands stuck deep in his trouser pockets below his waistcoat, swaying forward and backward as he spoke, bending over and then straightening himself; R. F. Scott's too descriptive word exactly represented it —'Heitland belly-ache-ing at the College meeting'. But in these later days he would fail to hear or to follow, and then withdraw. It was with an apology; he could not *hear*; so he would go, and (it was the October College meeting) he wished you all a happy Christmas and New Year; and was gone. Even in his prime he was a rather difficult colleague. 'Of all the terrible things I have known done in this room', he began at a Council meeting; so Scott said; and what did it lead up to? Why, said Scott, if I understood aright, they had rejected an amendment he moved. Again the sentence was famous, when the Council discussed remodelling the kitchen and its lane—there were the College servants to consider, and 'you may resent it or you may deplore it, but you cannot bridle their natural necessities'. I understand that the Council neither resented, nor deplored, nor attempted to bridle anything. If there was to be breakfast in the Combination Room, it might, said Scott, be planned to go on from 8 a.m. to 6 p.m., and then Heitland would turn up at 5.55 p.m., and if he did not find a sufficient supply of forks, things, we can believe, would be *pessimi exempli* and so forth. The reader perhaps will say that Scott must have had a certain gift of parody; survivors will be inclined to say there was very little parody in all this.

Something should be said of his versifying. When Oliver Wendell Holmes was entertained in the Combination Room, a poem, he says, was read to the gathering by a young Mr Heitland. It can be read in *The Eagle* of the time and some of it in Holmes's book *Over the Teacups*. But there was much else, e.g. a dreadful adaptation of the jingle in *Pickwick* to a famous lawsuit—

> Oh! Dilke, had you guessed
> How soon she'd confessed,
> When first your French vices you proffered—
> You'd have thought it more canny
> To stick to your Fanny,
> And leave Mrs Crawford to Crawford.

If he was vext with a man, he relieved his mind in metre for the moment—

> Or who so little prone to err
> As Dr D. MacAlister?

Other rhymes and jingles were kindlier. The song he wrote for Campbell College, Belfast, was admirable. Prose too served at times. His contributions to *The Cambridge Review*, however, at any rate in later years, were apt to be stiffly conceived, too cautious to let his native twinkle appear, as it did in conversation. He looked at you *over* his spectacles, with quick gleaming eyes— the brightest eyes in College (some one said J. R. Tanner smiled *underneath* his spectacles); and the quip came. There were more reasons than one, he grimly said (and didn't explain), why the camel is called the ship of the desert. When he heard of a Colonial University asking its professors to contribute heavily to the endowment of the chairs they held, it put them, he said, into the position of waiting to step into their own shoes.

He lived to a great old age, but, as he said on his last birthday, he 'didn't like being 86'. Illness, operation, and the Evelyn Nursing Home marked his last years. The legends of him at the Nursing Home chime in with those of College—sudden explosions of temper, and the nurse or the matron would sweep out of his room indignant, which of course *we* could not do. And yet, as one of the nurses told me, some of the staff, like his College colleagues, took the explosions quietly, and realized they were dealing with an extraordinary man, brilliant, clever, witty and essentially friendly, however surprising the sudden and short explosion. One recalls too the picture of Heitland allowed out of his room, moving slowly about the long corridor, crooning a hymn. Perhaps it was the last time I saw him, and character showed itself both ways. He lay abed in his own house, very far through, with a nurse sitting somewhere near. We spoke a little, and suddenly he made a terrible groaning. Shall I go? I said to the nurse. No! said she. In a moment Heitland looked at me—'A spasm', he said; and then the old humour asserted itself, and he quoted: 'And with the spasm all Erymanthus shook.' That was like him. Once I met him outside the Registry just as a magnificent Dean (a cathedral not a College Dean) was going in to pay a fee—a big-built handsome man whose figure was well set off by the dress. 'What would I not give', twinkled Heitland, 'to look like that? But', he added reflectively, 'I have always felt I was one of Nature's archbishops.' Here one may recall his saying that 'as a lay member of the Church of England, he was not obliged to believe the Creeds; but he was entitled to have clergy who did'. Another saying, relevant alike to morality and to University life; 'it takes a lot of virtues to make a good Vice'. Some Vice-Chancellors have forgotten it perhaps.

In his little autobiography *After Many Years*—a living sort of book, as you would expect—some trace appeared of old dissensions in College, notably a reference to a great 'injustice'. By this time there was nobody left, who could identify or explain the reference; so one must let it alone. But he was, as he admitted when the College gave him a dinner in the Combination Room on his eightieth birthday, somewhat severed from the College, and it was only 'the well-known bedside manner' of—we guessed whom—that had brought him. The younger men only knew him from his interjections at College meetings. It is perhaps relevant to say that after the dinner and the speech the old man walked home, a good mile on a December night. He left property to Newnham College and the University, so we have no monument to him as benefactor. An inscription was indeed written, and had the endorsement of his most intimate friend in College; but it has not been engraved.

M S

WILLELMI EMERTON HEITLAND SOCII

QUI

FACETIIS ABUNDANS

AMICIS FIDELIS

OFFENSARUM RARO NON MEMOR

MULTOS PER ANNOS

PARI ARDORE

COLLEGIUM COLEBAT

STUDIIS HISTORICIS INSTABAT

AMICITIAS INIMICITIASQUE

EXERCEBAT

NULLI NON

TERRORIS AUCTOR GAUDIIQUE.

II

If private loyalty dictates giving the first place to one's tutor, it is none the less the fact that in 1888, when I came into residence, the outstanding figure among Classical men at my College was Dr John Edwin Sandys. He was Public Orator, elected some twelve years earlier after one of the most exciting and prolonged election contests that the University had seen. The vacancy was declared in the Long Vacation when Jebb's removal to Glasgow was announced, and everything was done by both sides—everything lawful, that is, including special trains—to secure the victory, St John's on one side, Trinity on behalf of C. W. Moule then at Corpus on the other. On the election day many hundreds of graduates arrived to vote and in the end a decisive victory was won by Sandys and his friends (Sandys 701; Moule 587). But he was distinguished in other ways, as editor of the Classics and later on as author of the great standard *History of Classical Scholarship*. It was the book which won him his knighthood from Mr Asquith, who is reported to have spoken of the pleasure he felt in selecting Sandys and his satisfaction in that act at least; for, it seems, that the conferment of knighthoods does not add to the gaiety of a Prime Minister's life. There is at least a telling anecdote of Gladstone to that effect.

Sandys had been born in India, the son of a missionary. His mother had died when he was nine years old; her elder children had previously been sent to Europe, and John Edwin seems to have grown up a solitary child in a strange land, and serious beyond his years. For when, after a few years in Britain, he was to be sent to Repton, the young boy flung himself into the study of the history and archaeology of the region—a precaution that few schoolboys have taken. Heitland, I have said, was apt to be tragic; W. F. Smith leant to comedy; Sandys was neither tragic nor willingly comic; his character was marked by energy, concentration, a non-ebullient piety—and uneasiness. It was difficult for him to get on to an easy footing with pupil or colleague; and the real qualities of the man, which the years revealed, were too often hidden under a frigid and sometimes pompous manner. It was very unfortunate; it meant a polysyllabic stiffness, a propriety which often quite obscured the kindliness of his nature. There were constant tales of his remarkable utterances.

'I see', he said to a girl whose brother, as Fellow, had taken her into the Wilderness, 'I see you have been gathering some wild flowers, which is the legitimate privilege of all relatives of those who have access to the Wilderness.' Heitland would have said it shorter or not at all. Again to the same girl at some small tea party, handing him sugar (which had been delayed somehow). 'Oh! thank you,' he said; 'I always consider the first sip of tea taken without sugar as an opportunity irretrievably lost, for which no amount of subsequent sweetening' (the wicked Newnhamite stressed this alliteration when she told it) 'can ever atone.' There was some root of playfulness in that last remark, clearly, but the delivery made it seem unintentionally funny. So, when Leonard Whibley asked him when some new book of his was to be published, 'I believe', he said, 'that the publishers are even now casting the horoscope of its nativity'; and again the playfulness seemed to miscarry. Similarly, when he was not playful. In those days a fine English hexameter hung inside the College gate, very legible and conspicuous: 'Smoking is not allowed in the courts and grounds of the College.' And here was a little farewell scene at the end of term, a bunch of two or three men saying goodbye, and one of them was smoking. Down came Sandys (it was by accident, of course), and 'you know the rule', he said, 'about smoking; and yet you do it in the light of day and before the porters.' True, but the mixture of (let us say) the dying Ajax and the College servants made the wrong impression.

Sandys and his wife used to have Sunday afternoon At Homes —'perpendiculars', the graceless young used to call them, never thinking of the burden on host and hostess or the spirit that prompted the somewhat severe entertainment. The music was generally beyond and above us. Sandys moved about among the freshmen, and oddly seemed to know, and generally he mentioned, the staircase on which the men he introduced to ·each other 'kept'. A special friend of his was St J. B. Wynne Willson, a charming Classical scholar, afterwards Bishop of Bath and Wells. 'Do you know Mr Wynne Willson?' said Sandys to a freshman; he did; 'I congratulate you!' said Sandys. This reached College to the general delight. E. J. Brooks, Senior Classic, dashed headlong into Wynne Willson's rooms. 'I say, do you know Wynne Willson?' he demanded. Amazed, his host explained briefly that he was Wynne Willson—'I congratulate you!' said Brooks.

In the lecture-room it was much the same. The learning was immense, but it was uneasy. The fact is that writing and lecturing are different things. Let Sandys put his learning in a book, and it was apt to be a standard work; but lecturing requires selection, omission, concentration, and a human eye watching every reaction of the class; and Sandys, I think, abridged his material badly and would give the wrong emphasis—the detail, of course, was perfectly sound; Sandys was uniformly right in his facts—and, like some other learned and brilliant men, he was slow at reading an audience. The most brilliant lecturer I have known, an amazingly clever and amusing man, seemed to me most curiously insensitive to his audience; I shall mention his name in another chapter. In later years we had in Cambridge a great historian whom we read with delight; but without a manuscript he was apt to fumble heavily in the lecture room, and you might go further and say he murdered his own manuscript.

I have lingered long enough on the queer ways of Sandys, and I am rather sorry to do it, but it would not be Sandys without them. In spite of our youthful amusement at those ways, the years have added immensely to one's regard for him and one's gratitude to him. I was Heitland's pupil, of course; but Sandys told me he looked on me as a pupil of his own—'a friend'; and year after year bore witness to this kindness and goodness. If I may quote words used in the Senate House, when he received the honorary degree which he so well deserved—*Si discipulo talia licet confiteri, ex quo primum Collegio nostro interfui, hunc semper mihi comem recordor, semper jucundum, semper amicum fuisse.* He took me for walks, he included me in a little group that read Lessing's *Laocoon* in German at his house, he gave me books, he was greatly interested in my work, rejoiced in my successes, defended me in an hour of need (I won't give the particulars, but they were trying for the moment, funny in retrospect; and Sandys got them right). I was ill once for a spell, and, coming back to my room, I found Sandys' calling card with some good news on it, and a genial quotation from Pindar, ἄριστος Εὐφροσύνη πόνων κεκλιμένων ἰατρός. From the personal let me pass to the public services of the man.

Sandys was a scholar of a type which will never (one hopes) be quite extinct while human nature remains and while civilization and education have a place in this country, but it is not at all; commonly to be found in this generation as half a century ago. He was extraordinary, however, even among scholars of that day, at once for the width and the accuracy of his scholarship; he knew so much and knew it so well; he remembered everything with such precision, that it was dangerous to try to catch him tripping, and probably few people tried it twice. He had from the start a gift for writing Greek and Latin, both prose and verse, which is not very common among scholars and is to-day less cultivated than it once was. As a consequence, our scholarship has a good many loose edges, and fails in that exactness of knowledge which goes to make instinct, and on which, in the long run, everything depends. Sir John Sandys was not of the build of those who confine themselves to 'doing things more or less'; he was incapable of the untidiness of impressionism, and he took pains to know what he had to do.

Of his services to learning it is easy and not easy to speak. Few could say off-hand how many were the books he edited, standard as his editions remain of Isocrates and the speeches of Demosthenes. His edition of Euripides' *Bacchae* was famous; but other canons of interpretation prevail for the present, from which no doubt good results will follow, though not all said by modern exponents of the play will remain. He occupied his retirement by making a prose translation of Pindar for the Loeb Library, which has already seen a second edition. But his greatest work was the *History of Scholarship*—an achievement quite out of the range of most scholars. There are few to-day who could write a book to rival Mark Pattison's *Casaubon* and Monk's *Bentley*, and these were monographs. Sir John's history is encyclopaedic in its range; it is not lost in generalities, it gives pictures of men that are pictures, it is readable wherever you open it, and you can rely on what you read. It was not the least of his services to learning of every kind that when the Government, in the rage for efficiency, proposed to hand over the British Museum to a department of War Service, Sir John led the forces of sanity and learning which averted the risk and saved the Museum.

The records of his long tenure of the office of Public Orator are in his collected speeches. And here a little scandal will bring out the value of his work. Some time ago an ancient University of Scotland (be it nameless for the sake of decency) had a Fourth or a Fifth or Fourth-and-a-half Centenary, and Universities and seats of learning near and far sent addresses of congratulation, which were all published in a big volume. The addresses in Chinese and some other tongues were, I believe, lithographed to save anxiety to editor and printer; but the editors, to save their own faces and the printers', slipped in a little note to say that they had given the Latin addresses as they were received, though in some cases they had not quite understood the grammar and the constructions used by the senders. No such criticism was ever recorded—or made—of a speech or a letter written by Sir John and he wrote something like 700 or 800 for the Senate.

His death was in a way foreseen; it was known that he had heart trouble; but it came very suddenly. In July 1922 the present King, then Duke of York, and ex-President Taft were to receive

honorary degrees. I was putting on my gown to go to the Senate
House when my gyp came in, grave and disturbed: 'Sir John
Sandys has been taken ill in the Third Court.' I ran off and found
my old friend lying dead in his scarlet gown in a room near the
exit, Dr Shore and a gardener beside him; but all was over, and
with a merciful quickness. Some little time later, his friends put
up a brass to his memory in the College Chapel, where he had
worshipped for half a century.

IN PIAM MEMORIAM

JOHANNIS EDWINI SANDYS E Q

QUI DIU SOCIUS DIU TUTOR POSTREMO BENEFACTOR

COLLEGIUM ERUDITIONE ILLUSTRAVIT

ET LATINITATIS ORATOR PURISSIMAE

STUDIORUM ANTIQUORUM HISTORIAM CONSCRIPSIT

GRATO ANIMO POSUERUNT AMICI

MDCCCXLIV—MCMXXII

Let me add one word of esteem for the memoir written of him
by N. G. L. Hammond. Mr Hammond did not know him
personally, but using documents, letters and the testimony of his
friends, he has drawn a remarkably faithful portrait.

III

I now pass on to memories of C. E. Graves. Heitland, even
in the College of Peter Mason and John Mayor, was the most
startling character, and Sandys most famous among our scholars
for his learning and his effective books. (John Mayor knew heaps,
but no one would call his learning effective; it was all over the
place and gloriously irrelevant to most things.) Graves was easily
our most acceptable lecturer and teacher. Thus, when Aristotle's

Constitution of Athens was discovered, Sandys produced an edition of it out of sight more learned and more useful than the *editio princeps*; and he used his edition as a course of lectures. I was present at some of them; and one day he dictated to his class a table showing how various scholars dated the exiles and returns of Pisistratus. Eminently the thing for a note in his book, and as conspicuously (one would have said) not the thing for a lecture, and least of all for a lecture to youngsters, irrelevant to them, and (when all is said) dull. Graves was very different. Perhaps he was a shade indolent; perhaps (like some men) he lacked the spur of indigence; but he never wrote a big book—it has been suggested to me that not everybody *need* do this; there would be nobody to read if everybody wrote. He produced editions of Thucydides and Aristophanes for use in schools or by undergraduates. But when he was in the class-room, he knew where he was; and he spoke to the men in front of him. He was a scholar, and we saw it; he knew and cared for his authors; and he talked to the men who were there, and the class-room had normally a full attendance. No 'erm-nerm-ner' there, no oratory, no reading from proof-sheets; a scholar explaining an author and the author's language, and talking to men. And very human talk. He was dreadfully late one day, but he came in unperturbed, and mounted the platform—'Gentlemen, you must excuse me; the fact is, I was *sported out.*' I can hear his singular intonation yet, a lilt we tried to copy. The class-room applauded—loved him a little more, the human old dear—and the lecture began. He understood men better than did most of the dons, and, if I suggested that there was perhaps a certain indolence about him, it did not appear in his lectures, or in his criticism of our work; he was always awake and alert, dealing with the matter in hand. His criticisms were kindly; he never took the skin off; he never ripped your work and the fair copy to pieces as Haskins habitually did. If you did anything worth while, you saw he enjoyed it—not effusively, but naturally. There was a tranquil efficiency about him and a tranquil sense of humour.

Classical

Graves was walking with Heitland one day in the Backs, when they passed some one of whom Heitland disapproved. (That was easily possible.) Heitland growled:

> Whene'er I take my walks abroad,
> How many fools I see!

Graves murmured quietly in reply:

> And, maybe, what I thinks of them,
> They thinks the same of me.

A young lawyer was dining one night in hall. He talked all the time, chiefly about himself, and wound up by lamenting his shyness. Graves said sympathetically: 'I hope it does not stand in your way in your profession'; and the people sitting near felt that the balance was restored. To an old friend talking of daughters (they had each of them the same number): 'You've got to remember', said Graves, 'that you are their natural prey.' Once I heard him go a little further than usual. W. F. Smith turned up after some months of absence, bursting (like the happy schoolboy he was—a big plump and bearded schoolboy) with what he was doing. He was reading everything that Rabelais had ever read or quoted; to-day it had been 'Pope Innocentius *De Contemptu Mundi*'. But it did not stop there; and at last Graves murmured to me, '*Damn* Rabelais!' He and W. F. Smith were old schoolfellows; so I don't think he would have included Smith in Rabelais's doom, or anybody else either; but sometimes—at dinner, for instance—you can have too much Rabelais. I have felt the same thing myself when enthusiastic anthropologists have talked; e.g. an old missionary from Africa bitten by enthusiasm for *The Golden Bough*, and dilating for some courses on the treatment of the placenta by his natives. The subject was no doubt important and timely; but an indomitable frivolity of mind—I need confess no more, but that I was comparatively silent.

But I don't think that anybody can better what Graves wrote about himself—an 'epitaph', that was printed in some magazine,

the name of which I don't recall. It shows unusual knowledge of
himself, of his gifts and his range:

> Near where the Cam its margin laves
> Is laid the Reverend Mr Graves,
> Whom students reckoned at St John's
> Among the decent sort of Dons.
> His pupils always found him kind
> And to their faults a little blind.
> To learning he made small pretence
> But lectured plainly and with sense.
> As preacher he his help would lend
> Or read the prayers to serve a friend.
> Contented, and not apt to blame,
> He took things mostly as they came.
> He led an unassuming life
> And loved his children and his wife.
> He liked a pipe and modest glass,
> He liked to see a pretty lass.
> He did no harm, and, when he could,
> Maybe he did a little good.
> Of life he had a lengthy lease:
> Pray heaven his soul may rest in peace.

Yes! ὁ δ᾽ εὔκολος μὲν ἐνθάδ᾽ εὔκολος δ᾽ ἐκεῖ.

IV

W. F. Smith was, I now think, undervalued both by undergraduates and dons, Augustine Birrell (and not he alone) has
remarked as characteristic of Englishmen a certain suspicion that
tells against humour, if a public man possesses it; he may be
laughing at you, and, at any rate, a man who laughs cannot be
serious. Think for a moment of judges and magistrates and town
councillors; their success in life depends on nobody supposing
they would ever see, or ever make, a joke; and they don't. In old
days people did not like Mr Justice Darling, who appeared to
fancy himself as a humourist. W. F. Smith bubbled with humour,

laughed with you, told you funny things that had amused him, read and translated Rabelais. He lectured on Plautus and enjoyed it—enjoyed Plautus as comedy, and didn't seem to care very much for him as a document in the history of the Latin language. Preferred comedy to linguistic—no wonder we shook our grave young heads at him. And then Rabelais! "Ἀμήχανος γυνή—he (an undergraduate) translated it "a shiftless woman", and I said it was ambiguous, but he did not see the point.' Of course he didn't; it took an old Rabelaisian. The story went that he had said he blushed at some of the words he had to write in his translation of Rabelais. Nobody took that story too seriously, and some of the young saddled him with an opprobrious nickname—a name taken from a country public-house some miles out, once very notorious—most unjustly, as Graves indeed said. But Smith was light-minded. And then he was Steward of the College, and in charge of the kitchen. There have been a lot of stewards, chiefly botanists; and they have had to contend with dishonest employees now and then, with valuable old servants who would not contemplate a new idea ('look at his Chinese face', said one steward about his cook), with cockroaches, and juvenile dinner committees and their vague proposals of cheap food from Lyons. A brave steward later on swept the cockroaches, root and branch, out of the kitchen; what would the University Zoology laboratory do? asked one of the servants in dismay; it had always depended on our kitchen! But none of these things moved W. F. Smith; and at last there was revolt, led by William Bateson; Smith had not mastered the kitchen accounts and seemed unlikely to do it. So Bateson was set by the Council to manage the kitchen, and found the accounts quite perplexing enough; and Smith concentrated on Rabelais.

When composition and Plautus were no longer in the first line of our interests, perhaps others beside myself woke up to some sense of justice, and, like me, acquired the Rabelais. The value of his work was recognized; there was little question about that, though a not unkindly reviewer in *The Times* noted how the passion for annotation grew on him, as it does upon scholars. I have to own that I have often found more interest in W. F. Smith's notes than in Rabelais's text—that is perhaps a shocking confession. Smith's short book on Rabelais in his writings is a masterpiece of learning, relevance and compression; and it has been incorporated in the re-issue of his translation as an introduction. I think the student world can be far too practical, and I fancy that their tutors encourage this. The object of a University course is undoubtedly a good degree, only to be obtained by success in examinations; and year after year the undergraduate asks himself and his friends whether the stuff they hear in this and the other lecture-room will be set in the Tripos; all depends on that. There was no question about Rabelais coming into our Tripos. Everything that Graves gave us might come in; so we ranked his lectures as better than Smith's, and probably they were —*ad hoc* as Englishmen say. But, as I look back, it is with the feeling that you gain something from a teacher who has interests that do not *a priori* concern you; he may liberate your mind, may give you new ideas, open new fields of study. So W. F. Smith remains in affectionate memory, no doubt of that—twinkling, and babbling, and bubbling—and intermittently in his genial way suggesting your limitations (not to pain you!) and heading you for scholarship more clearly than you recognized, and reminding you not too obtrusively that literature is more than scholarship.

V

C. E. Haskins was a great contrast to Graves and W. F. Smith. A quick agile man, with a certain jerkiness in mind and action. The story was told of a plunge he made in the Combination Room and the cup of coffee suddenly flung over Heitland's trousers. Heitland, however, took the accident genially; it was in view of such contingencies, he suggested, that he wore trousers. We were afterwards told of his general judgment on Haskins as 'a good fellow, but when he has a cup of coffee in his hands, I don't want to be anywhere near him'. They worked together, however, in producing the edition of Lucan. Heitland, as I have said, wrote the very searching and drastic introduction; Haskins did the commentary—'no sufficient literary evidence of his powers', wrote Heitland six years later, after his premature death; 'his work on Lucan was hurried over too fast to do him full justice'. But even the savage Housman, denouncing the commentary as 'unlearned', admits it is 'not wanting in common sense'. The book, long out of print, is still catalogued by the booksellers at a fairly high price.

But Lucan did not represent Haskins altogether. As I write, my mind goes back to the class-room, and Haskins lecturing. From one point of view, he was one of the worst lecturers I ever heard, always 'stammering and gasping' as a limerick about him said, the fact being truer than the rhyme. During one of these lectures W. C. Summers, afterwards professor at Sheffield and a scholar of high gifts, especially interested in the Silver Age of Latin, knocked off a verse and gave it me:

> A dauntless nine to Haskins came,
> Half-dead they went away;
> But high in list was each man's name
> When lists came out in May.

Read June for May, and look up the Tripos lists; and you will find that in one year and another, three of the dauntless nine achieved 'i, 1'—first division of the first class. It meant that the stronger men came to the terrible lectures, if the weaker stayed away. Haskins, we used to say, when he lectured, never finished a sentence; he would make five shots at it, fill in the gaps with an odd refrain of his own—'erm-nerm-ner'; and then abandon the proposed sentence, leaving you to divine what he was after, and going on to something else. But he was a real teacher. The matter was 'piece-y', as people say now; the form was shattered; the delivery was dreadful; but there you had a man, with interests and ideas, alive and alert, and they were not humdrum or conventional ideas. He did not choose the usual books of school and

58 *Classical*

class-room as his themes. We owed to him our introduction to
Suetonius and Polybius—dreadfully dull authors, some would
say; but no! there were living interests tangled up with 'erm-
nerm-ner', and we were brought into new fields of ancient life,
very profitably. Heitland records the verdict of Tripos examiners
upon the high standard reached in Ancient History by Haskins's
pupils; 'no wonder', he ejaculates; 'for their teacher threw his
heart into his work and had them constantly in his thoughts'.
Genial vehemence and unaffected loyalty were the qualities his
colleague emphasized in him; and a pupil can subscribe to it. He
was a drastic critic and a good friend, a man of strong opinions,
who could differ without quarrelling. After eighteen or nineteen
years of College teaching, a sudden illness carried him off in three
days. It is long ago since we went to those explosive lectures, but
I am conscious in retrospect of what they did for me. Other men
lectured to me on Tacitus, Demosthenes, Sophocles; I have not
attempted those authors; but I did try the book of Suetonius to
which Haskins introduced us (the *Augustus*), and Polybius has
long been an absorbing study, years after poor Haskins died so
prematurely.

VI

My first attempt at book production was not as author, but (if
I may borrow a rather big phrase) as 'only begetter' of H. R.
Tottenham's collected works. R. F. Scott joined in, and supplied
copies of some of them that he had saved; but I remember
that he was not precisely pleased at my entrusting them to 'Tottie',
as we called him; he would do nothing with them. But he did;
and I still treasure the little grey book with the inscription on the
fly-leaf: 'To T. R. Glover, without whose kindly offices in the
double capacity of μύωψ and μαῖα (to say nothing of νάρκη) this
little book might not have seen the light, from the Author June
1st 1895.'[1]

1 The Greek words signify gadfly and monthly nurse, terms used by
Socrates, while νάρκη is the electric eel.

Harry Rede Tottenham came to us from Trinity—our first adoption (at any rate in the ages that I know about) of an out-College man. He had in 1879 been bracketed Senior Classic with E. V. Arnold, afterwards professor in Wales and an authority on Roman Stoicism. Tottenham had also been Porson scholar, Craven scholar and first Chancellor's medallist. After his migration, his life as lecturer among us was considerably less strenuous. Everybody liked him, but nobody would have called the picturesque, untidy humourist an energetic character. With his pupils he was shy, hesitant in the lecture-room, and in his own room face to face perhaps shyer still, nervously hinting errors in their work or stammering of possible improvements they might adopt, but always with a curious little smile of his own coming and going, and winning him goodwill. Tottenham (this isn't really important, you will say—unless you are a little grateful to Pliny for telling you that Scipio Aemilianus was the first Roman to shave every day) was alone among the Classical teachers of my youth in being beardless. Our High Table had at the time, I suppose, more beards than the whole University could produce to-day; it was not yet considered courteous or humorous to shout 'Beaver!' at a man with a beard. (I could imagine it was Oxford that taught us that habit.) In those days, and indeed later, dons could be very great and solemn; he was not either. Congratulating a pupil on his degree, he jerked out: 'Of course we all expected it; but examiners are sometimes asses.' Not everybody was so explicit in those days about examiners and the sacred Tripos. A place or two in the list might win you or lose you a College living. And the purest of 'pure scholarship' still prevailed, complicated by a pathetic love of Grammar and its terms, and a still more irrelevant one for Philology, which was supposed to be a science and was as dogmatic then—or nearly—no! not quite—as Psychology is to-day.

If I correctly gauge Tottenham's own attitude to Grammar and Philology, they did not supremely interest him; and his friends did not suffer in consequence. He was not of the type that gives great commentaries to the world; he was as remote as you could imagine from the Jebb and Sandys order. But he would, under stimulus of his friends, write an article for *The Eagle* or *The Cambridge Review*, full of curious Classical learning, taken as it were sideways. He was the scholar who identified the easy form of divorce used by the Romans—*solvuntur risu tabulae; tu, Missus, abibis*. It was a collection of these brilliant papers which formed the book of which I spoke, and he entitled it (borrowing the name from Juvenal) *Cluvienus His Thoughts*—Cluvienus being nobody in particular. The dedication was interesting. He was our Praelector, or in the old phrase 'Father of the College' for degree-day purposes. So he dedicated his book: 'Coll. Div. Joh. Pater Adoptivus Optimo Mediocris.'

The book perhaps appeals most of all to Classical men, for Aristotle and Pindar are not widely read in other schools. It is full of indebtedness to Aristotle, as is seen in the article on the Magnificent Man and in the Nicomachean Ethics of Whist—subjects a good deal more amusing in Tottenham's hands than in the original. His absurdity always comes with a serious look and with bursts of sheer irrelevance gravely introduced. The ideal whist-player is defined in Aristotle's own way (for virtue lies in the mean) as the mean between the heroic card-sharper and the bumble-pup. The game recurs through the book, and Dr Verrall is told in the delightful letter addressed to him that he has 'no enemies except your partner for the time being'. *The Cambridge Review* had a series of 'Letters to Lecturers', but this eclipsed the lot. It is in this that he gives the famous Horatian description of Verrall as *splendide emendax*. The 'Notes on an Old World Play' are again a parody of Verrall, dealing with Punch and Judy—'*my* opinion for whatever it is worth, is that in this drama we have a type of the purification of the human soul, till, as personified in Punch, it utters its triumphant cry of victory over the conquered passions and distractions of the world of sense. In the murder, then, of (1) Judy and the child, (2) the Doctor, and (3) the Executioner, I seem to see the story of the struggle of the soul to free itself from the bonds of (a) family, (b) social, and (c) political ties, and in self-centred exaltation to rise to communion with the great sky-father.'

The Epinikian ode to the Agricultural Voter recalls the General Election of 1885 and Joseph Chamberlain's war-cry of 'three acres and a cow', but the scholar will find it Pindaric *in excelsis*, full of gorgeous original Pindarisms and others taken from the poet himself as gorgeously misapplied. There is a footnote, too, on the famous 'Whetstone' passage 'which drags me on with flowing blasts'—a note required, for 'Böckh reads "sidles up to me" which seems more in consonance with what we know of the habits of whetstones'. The Thucydidean boat-captain addresses his crew and urges that 'that boat, which has fewest distinct times in it, will be successful in most points'. 'Cambridge as she is visited' was a burlesque of a famous Portuguese handbook to English speech. It consisted of 'familiar dialogues and idiotisms'. The luncheon-room episode at the station will suffice. 'Have you any pullet, Miss? give me immediately a stick's drum, some bosom and the lights inwards on a proper plate; also a lamprey, any garlic, some citrons and a bottle of Oporto wine. Hark, the guardsman who puffs his horn. "All the world to the vehicle." Here is a bill of exchange.' The 'Highest Locals' are reported on, with a Platonic motto: 'The un-examined life is not live-able by man'; and we learn that in French 'many marks were lost by candidates knowing nothing about the subject', while in Greek the one candidate 'knew more parts of *tupto* than the Ancients and satisfied the Examiner'. There was verse in the volume, and in the Jubilee Ode William Bateson's investigations of the effect on shellfish of differing degrees of salinity in lakes near the Caspian or some such region receive honourable mention. (This work was done in his pre-Mendelian days.)

> Where cold *Sarmatia* spreads her cloak of snow,
> A son of *John's*—where will not *Johnians* go?—
> Essays t' unravel *Nature's* tangled skein,
> And trace their denizens from *Lake* to *Main*;
> The finny brood grow salt by slow degrees,
> And pickled salmon swim th' astounded seas.

Not all Tottenham's contributions to the gaiety of College life were printed in that book. There were limericks which acquired a wide currency; the two best known were about the Rev. Edwin Hill, one of the tutors in my earlier years, and in each case the poet, like Shakespeare, incorporated the prose that lay to his hand, and all he did, as Heine put it in Shakespeare's case, was to put the soul in it that made it alive. Hill had expressed his feeling for Cambridge, though he later on abandoned the University for a College living; but Tottenham immortalized him:

> There once was a Tutor, whose piety
> Made him careless of change or variety;
>   'In all England', quoth he,
>   'I hold Cambridge to be
> The most pleasant provincial society.'

Then there had been a discussion in the Senate, in which Hill took part, was (as he thought) misconceived, and rose with a correction; and once more the minimum of change put him into verse:

> There was a strong man on a Syndicate
> Who loved the exact truth to vindicate;
>   He rose to deny
>   That his words could imply
> What their sense seemed intended to indicate.

One of the saddest things about the New World University is the quality of its nonsense. The English statesman was right who demanded if some man discussed was capable of nonsense; and there is much in Henry Sidgwick's question, 'But is it the right kind of nonsense?' It may be the low standard of the Classics in America, or Standard Oil, and other earnest enthusiasms that we must blame. There is much in a Canadian's judgment that the mark of American humour is exaggeration and of English under-statement. 'The worst of me', said Mark Twain, 'is that I exaggerate so; it is the only way I can approximate to the truth.'

Chapter III

OUT COLLEGE

I

In my youth a man was taught in his own College. There were brilliant lecturers at Trinity, but one was not sent to them. No one ever suggested that such men as Jackson and Verrall, or among the professors Westcott and Seeley, might be worth hearing, at least once. This was a mistake; for with years I am more and more clear that the significant man does more for a pupil by his mere personality than a dozen lectures full of useful information dictated by an ordinary person, however correct; and most College lecturers are ordinary people. For instance, I constantly think of two lectures by Rendel Harris that I heard —I might say that I watched; for his Woodbrooke audience, gathered from Britain, the United States, Holland and Norway, with stray people of other origins and abodes, was part of it. He took two hours (on separate days) to give us what a commonplace person would have told us in ten minutes or less; only in that case it would probably all have been forgotten; as it was, it was an experience, and a landmark. The whole class was enlisted, and there and then worked the matter out. The question was the date of Christ's birth, and we all started calculating about Cyrenius and the year of the Greeks and so forth, the orthodox ones never guessing that they were engaged in Higher Criticism; it was all so natural, right and inevitable.

But my immediate subject is a Cambridge retrospect, so, to go back to 1889, an exception was made in favour of Jebb, whose lectures I once discussed before the Classical Association. I gained very little from them; and, as I said, I found in later Canadian days that my colleague, James Cappon, a most able and contributive

man to whom I owe much, had the same sense of missing
Sophocles after a whole winter in Glasgow of Jebb on the play or
plays. Jebb, like some others at whom I have hinted, was more
useful in print.

More stimulating, at least to me—far more—were the lectures
of an old schoolfellow, Leonard Whibley of Pembroke. He was
six years my senior, a big boy at school when I was little, though
time reversed our bodily proportions. He was elected a Fellow
not long after my coming to Cambridge; and all along he supported me with guidance, criticism, solid sense and freakish nonsense. In particular he brought me into acquaintance with two
outstanding Pembroke men—R. A. Neil, Aberdonian, scholar,
Sanskritist, most lovable of men; and the eccentric Heriz Smith,
famous for trying as Proctor to discipline a Jesus man with
'penance' instead of a fine, and famous too as the central figure
of the 'Belly-banders'. These men, so called from the sash they
wore on ceremonial occasions, were a 'very dangerous' High
Church group, devoted to nobody knew what theological de-
signs—really, I think, devoted to Heriz Smith, who was interesting enough to tempt any one to wear a 'belly-band'. They
discussed all sorts of things (I was told)—wild heresies (as heresies
then went); and then, to conclude the evening (I am told) Heriz
Smith would wind up the meeting with the nervous suggestion
that 'we can all at least unite in reciting the Apostles' Creed'.
Well, it was something to lunch with such men at Whibley's.
But he did more. I was no doubt to take the Second Part of the
Classical Tripos; then why not the History section? He was to
lecture in 1890–91 on the Greek Law subject (an appalling in-
gredient which people then thought significant in Greek History);
why should I not come to the lectures, and see how the section
appealed to me?

I went to the lectures: and, of course, I took the History section,
and it gave a bent to my whole life. The subject that year was a
lucky one; for Greek Law is not always gay. But the litigation of
Apollodorus with his stepfather (all preserved in the so-called

Private Speeches of Demosthenes, though some of them Apollodorus wrote himself) was at once full of human interest—banking, slavery, marriage, navy and knavery, perjury and so on—and the law involved had interesting and inglorious complications. Years later I had to lecture on the same subject myself, and my foundation was Whibley, and a very sure foundation. He became assistant secretary to the University Press, and at a lunch, at which Neil was the other guest, he broached the scheme of a school edition of Demosthenes' *Olynthiacs*. I can see Neil's quiet laughter as Whibley unfolded the most golden prospects of preposterous royalties. So I 'commenced author', as they used to say, or at least editor; and then came a startling coincidence. The Macmillans had simultaneously asked Dr Sandys to edit the same speeches for the same purpose. It was like the old friend to write to our Press, to say that this competition was undesigned. So both books came out; the earthen pot, so to speak, was not hit by the metal one; my little book was sold out, and the Press proposed to reprint it, but I thought it had served its day and might cease to be. Rendel Harris had warned me that, if I did another school book, he would 'give me up'! That was not to be faced. In later years Whibley made an attempt to translate Thucydides, without using the flowing English of Jowett, which he, like some other critics, found sufficiently unlike the actual Thucydidean style; but, after doing two books, he decided the thing was impossible. He was better employed, in a great edition of Thomas Gray's letters, taken over when Paget Toynbee died; a congenial task, in which he was eminently successful.

So Whibley headed me into Ancient History, and I may well be grateful. I don't know what study would have given me more variety of interests or more human values. I was launched now into a whole series of out-college lectures. I went to James Smith Reid, afterwards Professor of Ancient History, a most learned and acute Latinist, constantly quoted by A. S. Wilkins in his Horace and by other learned editors; a most kindly man; but he gave his pupils little zest for Roman Law. He wrote a big book afterwards

on the Roman municipalities, and made a great mistake—or his
publishers did it for him, a tribe terribly awake to ways and means,
to the costs of production and the improbability of sales; for he
suppressed all references to his authorities. If he reached a second
edition, he told me he meant to add them; but he died in old age
before that came. On Roman History I went to A. A. Tilley, who
did his work conscientiously and fully; it was of value to us as an
introduction to the period, but it somehow lacked inspiration.
Perhaps it was because, like others of those who taught me, Tilley
was looking elsewhere—not indeed to Rabelais with the exclusive
passion of W. F. Smith, but to the French Renaissance which
occupied his later years. He never, so far as I know, published
anything on the period of Cicero.

More significant, by far, were the lectures of J. W. Headlam on
the early period of Greek History. Like Whibley he had won a
Prince Consort essay prize; and Whibley's *Political Parties at
Athens* and Headlam's *Election by Lot* were long outstanding
among prize essays—yes, and among books that had not that
dubious label—so outstanding that one's friends borrowed them,
and one never saw them again—that sort of book. Headlam
fascinated me. They were long-drawn lectures, with a wide
range; the Greek of the period touched so many lands and seas
and races; and the authors were so interesting. He set us reading
Herodotus, not in driblets, but from cover to cover, and introduced us to Strabo and Pausanias; and all three have been authors
beloved and read through later years—a possession for ever, if
I may turn the Greek critic's phrase over to the credit of his rival.
One *had* to read up a certain amount of Roman Law, and no end
of material from Gaius Gracchus to the Rubicon; and I don't say
it was distasteful; but it was Headlam's Greek period that was a
delight to delve in, and so it has remained, while my sentiment
for Roman Law is what Englishwomen call Platonic, lacking the
element of passion. I was lucky in Whibley and Headlam.
Headlam's later story is interesting too; he turned to Germany,
married there, wrote on Germany; drifted into Foreign Office

service, acquired a double-barrelled name, was knighted; and it was he, who, rightly or wrongly, was credited with inventing or re-discovering Danzig as a Free Town, an unfortunate application of ancient history. But, as I say, Headlam counted in my life, and was a factor for good.

II

After my degree, other teachers supervened—H. M. Gwatkin and Rendel Harris.

Gwatkin stood easily at the head of the Cambridge lecturers whom I regularly heard. His subject was Church History, and he knew it in and out, back and forth, root and branch—the original authorities and the secondary. He had a thought-out position, a very definite one; people who differed from him called it bias—a word that serves wonderfully well in human affairs and saves no end of trouble that might have to be expended on evidence and argument; for one is never biased oneself. He knew what he meant to say—during the term and in the immediate lecture; he had a strong sense of values, of proportion and perspective; and he drove for the central issues. Some lecturers digress charmingly, and some get lost in insignificant detail. Gwatkin knew where he was going and kept to his direction. He had a sense of form, too; and it was all alive—even thrilling now and then. Like St Augustine preaching, Gwatkin lecturing was content with a half-sheet of notes or headlines; and he *talked* his lecture, but he never got lost. On the contrary, I made the curious discovery that year by year, lecturing from notes, his sentences might be the same; and I rather fancy that close study would reveal some of them in the two volumes he published on Early Church History. People, of course, said you had to 'learn the language'; for Gwatkin had been deaf from childhood and he had a deaf man's intonations. It took a lecture or two to get into his speech; and then—what lectures they were! He would challenge his class to go to the original authorities and prove him wrong;

I took up his challenge—in no hostile spirit—and I have the note-book still, interleaved, rebound, and full of notes and references of my own gathering. The lectures and the reading occupied much of my time between 1892 and 1896, when I left England; and it meant an immense gain in outlook and interests.

But there was more. Gwatkin took classes on the original authorities. It was to one of these I first went—an evening class. Hours of hall differ in different Colleges, and though I went straight off from dinner to Emmanuel, where he was lecturing, I was a few minutes late. There was a roomful of men, and the grey-haired, grey-bearded lecturer, whom I had never seen before, was striding about. He always strode up and down when he lectured. As I entered, he and all of them turned on me. 'Have *you* a Tacitus?' he demanded. Of course I hadn't—I had not heard it was wanted—and the class unanimously laughed. Then we settled down to *Annals* xv, 44. So it went on, week by week, on Tuesday nights; but before long Gwatkin shifted the hour, to allow (I supposed) a pupil from St John's High Table to get there in time. Men fell away; and one night, when I reached the room, Gwatkin was pacing up and down alone. He looked up, as I entered; 'I thought you would come.' It was clear that I was to be his only hearer; so I begged him not to trouble to lecture; but no! he would, and he did; and I have always felt bound to do as he did. We often walked back to his house after those evening lectures; and I think of the room lined with books, the cabinet full of the tongues of *radulae* (molluscs) which he loved to dissect (for he was a great zoologist, with a special field)—and lastly the favourite cat on the mantelpiece. When his portrait was put in his last book, he had a cat in his arms.

He too, like so many of my teachers, was from Shrewsbury, a pupil of Benjamin Hall Kennedy. But he suffered under him, for Kennedy insisted on daily 'rep'—so many lines of Virgil, or whoever it might be, by heart. Gwatkin had a tremendous memory for facts and dates, but he had no gift for learning things by heart. He could not trust himself, he said, to repeat the Lord's

Prayer in public without book. So the 'rep' cost him hours, and in his case it was of little value. Of course we, who were young, found oddities in Gwatkin; the book he was writing was always 'pestiferous'; smoking was—well, he would ask one to dine at a feast at Emmanuel, and after dinner there was to be 'a great stink' for which he would commit you to 'learned and odoriferous hands'. Public lectures, text-classes, endless private talk, guidance in reading, criticism of outlooks and impressions, sheer friendship and constant help—once more it all illustrates what I want to emphasize, that the real University, the real College life, is the contact of minds, more often achieved over a friend's fire, or on the Grantchester meadows, than in a class-room. In this case I had both—*Deo gratias*. And let me brag a little—or no! I won't; you can turn up the last words of the preface of Gwatkin's Church History. But I will add what is characteristic. I read a great mass of his proofs in slip on the train one day; posted them in Norwich station; and by the time I reached Sheringham, wondered if I had commented too freely. So I wrote to him, and I had a reply that revealed him. The only thing he had against my criticisms of his book was—would I please use a blacker pencil.

III

It was an even closer intimacy, and a longer one, with Rendel Harris. I had not been long in Cambridge before I met people who talked to me about him. He was at that time in the United States, but his memory was cherished with a peculiar loyalty. He had had one Cambridge career already and was to have another. He was from Plymouth, one of a large family—eleven children— sprung of a yet larger one of twenty-two; and among his first cousins were Lord Rendel, Gladstone's friend, and Austin Dobson, the poet and essayist, friend of all who study the eighteenth century, than which there are few better studies. Rendel Harris was born in 1852, and early took to Mathematics, which led to Cambridge, a high Wranglership, and a Fellowship at Clare. He became a Mathematical lecturer, and was nominated by his College to be 'Moderator' in the Mathematical Tripos, in which capacity he had to assess the merits of Joseph Larmor and J. J. Thomson, and with his colleagues brought out Larmor Senior Wrangler and 'J. J.' second. Larmor became a Fellow of St John's, secretary of the Royal Society, Lucasian Professor and M.P. for the University; and it has been one of the happiest things in my College life, that he was one of my most intimate friends, constantly making gentle fun of me, and as constantly proving a real support in all sorts of things. A bachelor, he lived just across the second court and had the gift of being at leisure when one looked in.

Rendel Harris—like two other Mathematicians in my acquaintance, Charles Taylor, Master of St John's, to whom the University Library owes the famous Genizeh Collection from Egypt, and Professor F. C. Burkitt—turned over to Theology and Semitic languages, especially in his case Syriac. So he left Clare and Cambridge, and taught one of his new subjects at Johns Hopkins University in Baltimore, till some academic disagreement (perhaps about vivisection) led to his removing to the pleasant Quaker College of Haverford, a delightful place in wooded grounds, a real 'campus', some miles outside Philadelphia. And then about 1890 he returned to Cambridge, to lecture on Palaeography, and was re-elected a Fellow of Clare for six years. When the six years had passed, he was continued for four, and after that for two; and then, he said he knew what Arithmetical Progression was, and, a call to Woodbrooke near Birmingham coinciding, he left us for ever—not to the gain of Cambridge. Meanwhile he had lectured here for years, and for a long time I went to his class in Palaeography, a class like no other. We were older and younger men, and among us were Mrs Lewis and Mrs Gibson, the discoverers of the Sinai Syriac MS. Every one was given, lecture by lecture, a photograph of some page of MS.; and the rule was that whoever first caught the initial word should read on till he or she blundered, and the turn passed to whoever caught them out. It was great fun, a real adventure, and (it is to be remarked) it was doing the actual thing itself, not hearing about it, though, of course, we did hear about it, the brilliance and wit of Rendel Harris playing over all the work. It was real work and real wit; and we were consorting with a genius. This continued till he went to Woodbrooke, in which he, H. G. Wood and R. S. Franks (both Cambridge men, too) were the formative factors. Afterwards he had years at the Rylands Library in Manchester.

I do not know how often he was in the Nearer East. He went to Armenia with his wife, to learn at first hand what Abdul Hamid was doing to the Armenians. Mrs Harris was not a bloodthirsty woman—she was in fact a tranquil Quakeress—but when, in Scarborough in 1897, I heard her speaking of what they had learnt in Armenia, I felt that if, in the phrase of Tertullian rendered by Gibbon, I could see Abdul Hamid 'liquefying in fiercer flames than ever he had kindled against the Christians', I would feel a very non-Quakerish exaltation. It was not to be. Abdul Hamid had another end, 'rightly rewarded'. But beside atrocities there were other interests. Rendel (his friends didn't say Harris very much) wrote to me of 'bathing in that sweet river of Paradise, the Hiddequel'—in modern maps the Tigris, but it was like him to prefer Genesis to Kiepert and Bartholomew. He loved the picturesque, the allusive phrase; on one of my voyages to Canada, he engaged to 'fan my sails with Zephyrs, laden with orisons'. (I hope the orisons came on a more Easterly wind.) Every here and there he fell in with MSS., generally Syriac, which led to two significant discoveries. In one of his MSS. he found a Syriac translation of the lost Greek apology for Christianity which was known to have been written by Aristides in the second century. This was a great find, and he arranged with Armitage Robinson to print it in the *Texts and Studies*, which Robinson was then editing. While it was in the press, Robinson happened to be reading the curious romance called *Barlaam and Josaphat*; and in this he came on a defence of Christianity, which struck him as somehow familiar; where could he have seen it? He suddenly thought of Rendel Harris's proofs, caught them up, and found he had discovered the Greek original, cribbed entire and incorporated by the much later novelist. So between them Aristides stepped back into Christian literature, to a place he deserved.

Many years later, a dismal winter day kept Rendel a prisoner in his study at Selly Oak. To relieve monotony he turned to his book-shelves; every scholar is apt to forget his acquisitions, and it is profitable to go over them from time to time. He took down a Syriac MS., which he thought was a Psalter, the Psalms of David; but it was not. Suddenly, in the Uncle Remus phrase that he loved to quote, he 'fotch up on his behime legs'; it was no Psalter of David's, but Solomon's. He had found another lost book, a complete MS. of the *Odes of Solomon*—not that King Solomon wrote them; they are not the least like the Proverbs or Ecclesiastes, but Christian hymns of a mystical character and of some real beauty. Bound up with them was a Syriac translation of the *Psalms of Solomon*, quite another type of thing—a Jewish psalter, in which Pompey's invasion of the Temple and his well-deserved end are mentioned; the Greek of these had long been familiar.

But the *Odes* made a great sensation among scholars all over the world. And then a wonder came to light; for after an interval F. C. Burkitt found that long before this the learned William Wright had catalogued among Syriac MSS. in the British Museum another copy of the identical book, though it had not interested Wright nor attracted the least notice. Some things are spiritually discerned, and it took Rendel Harris to see the beauty of the little poems, their tenderness of Christian feeling, which made his own heart burn within him. I happened to be with Rendel when he ran into Solomon Schechter, the great Hebrew scholar—big, untidy, brilliant—in the University Press office. They greeted and speedily reached the *Odes*, and Schechter said he could not place them in Judaism. And their date? Could they really belong to the first century A.D.? If they did, the great

German scholar Julicher was quoted as saying, 'then all our criticism of the Fourth Gospel is *kaput*'.

Though not bred a Quaker, Harris had joined the Society of Friends; but 'convinced friend', as he was, he remained in far warmer sympathy with the Free Churches and evangelical religion than is common in that Society. An early Quaker editor of John Woolman's Journal took the precaution of deleting the name of Christ in many places, and substituting 'God'—a manœuvre in scholarship and Theology, of which Rendel Harris was quite incapable. He wrote a number of devotional books, the first and most famous, his *Memoranda Sacra*, a collection of addresses delivered in the Friends' Meeting at Cambridge, which a friend had taken down. Perhaps even better was his *Guiding Hand of God*. His *Woodbrooke Litanies*, dealing with the falling leaf, the skylark, and kindred themes, were a sore trial to self-conscious literalists who had to join in reciting them, but for others they were full of the happy charm of their author—things no other hand on earth could have written. Large part of the appeal of his writing and of his speech lay in the range of reading brought to bear, the quaintness and unexpectedness of allusion and interpretation, the gaiety of phrase for which nothing was 'sacred' and yet everything was sacred in a real sense, the bright friendliness of glance, and the deep happiness of assured peace with God.

Those who only read his books perhaps never knew to the full his gift for nonsense. 'What's the evidence?' I asked him about some new theory which he was advancing. He answered very gravely: 'It rests on something better than evidence.' I opened my eyes; and he went on as gravely: 'Conjectural emendation.' Sometimes the theory did rest on conjecture. In reading again since his death a number of his learned works, I have felt uneasily that many of his propositions wanted more proof than he gave them; and I am since told that, long before, Dr Hort had made the criticism that Harris seemed insufficiently conscious of alternatives. But there was a lot in Foakes Jackson's suggestion that men like Rendel Harris and Verrall have to reckon on a certain number of their ideas being inevitably wrong; Jackson suggested 30 per cent. Suppose it had been more—you gain something from the wider knowledge and the quicker wit—something more valuable than a correct conclusion—a heightened sense of latent problems, of questions yet to be asked; and it makes for fuller life of the mind. Once—you may count this rather priggish—I asked myself what I really owed to Rendel Harris; and the answer was, not this, nor that, nor the other thing, but just this that for years I had talked over with him everything that interested me and found it more interesting than I had supposed, while his interests were always opening up new avenues of thought, and if some of them had dead ends, some, like the folklore of twins, had not. He was bold to recklessness, quick beyond words to catch an unsuspected value, a man of range and memory and suggestion beyond the common—a friend, a scholar, a humourist, a fighter (Quaker, too!) and a saint.

During the last twelve or fifteen years of his life he was very much the invalid. Trouble with his sight involved the removal of one eye, but it did not dismay him; no, he was now, like a certain Gospel figure, to enter the Kingdom of Heaven 'having one eye'; and meanwhile he would enjoy 'the monophthalmic view of life'. Toward the end the other eye failed, but the spirit did not.

All told, I think I have been happy in my friends outside the College.

IV

Other men outstanding among the Classical scholars of Cambridge I came to know after my return from Canada.

There was A. W. Verrall, for instance. I knew him first as chairman of the Tripos examiners, when I first examined—a very brilliant and amusing man, but not an ideal chairman. He took over a scheme from the previous year for the allotment of work, which acted with quite remarkable unevenness; all the heaviest work fell on the two juniors, H. J. Edwards of Peterhouse and me.

I do not suggest that this was Verrall's intention; but I cannot help recalling that, when by some chance on the General paper the lighter sections came to Edwards and me, one of the senior men squealed, and announced that this seemed unfitting, and it ought to be done over again. Verrall did not surrender to him; and I recall Peter Giles's occasional comment when this old gentleman expressed himself about the work. 'Sugar!' was all he said. With Verrall and Heitland at the top of the table, there were brighter moments at our meetings. One of Verrall's shots stays with me. A piece of Thucydides had been set and the text fought over; at last those interested decided what to print. The voice of Verrall was heard declaring that the words to be printed conveyed nothing to an ordinary mind. The colleague, who provoked Giles's 'sugar', rejoined that he saw no great difficulty in it. 'Ah! my dear Blank', shrilled Verrall, 'I said "an ordinary mind".' This was an alleviation—this inversion of their roles; for nobody ever credited Verrall with an ordinary mind, and it would have been the utmost that anybody would have allowed to the other man.

Verrall's books need no comment of mine. I always recall the exhilaration of reading his study of Horace for the first time, but I had not the same sensation when I went back to it some years later. But the great occasion was when Verrall lectured on *The Birds* of Aristophanes, which he demonstrated to be a parody of what he politely called 'Palestinian religion'. It was amazingly ingenious, and I listened rapt. I met Whibley next day, who laughed about it; 'Did you ever consider', he asked me, 'that Prometheus might be John the Baptist?' I had not, as a matter of fact. And then a strange thing occurred. Whether Verrall read from a MS. (as I rather think) or was taken down verbatim, the lecture was to appear on the following Thursday in *The Review*, and it didn't. Verrall had suddenly withdrawn it, and the supplement was destroyed—all but one copy, which the editor of the year kept. Long afterwards this was produced, set up again and published; but alas! it was not so splendid to read as to hear. But the comment of *The Cambridge Review* stands—'se non è vero, è Verrall.'

A little bit more about Verrall and the *Birds*. Somewhere about that time F. M. Cornford produced his book *Thucydides Mythistoricas*. It was in two parts. In the second he gave his judgment on Thucydides as a historian, making me for one recall Matthew Arnold's quip about Stopford Brooke in his History of English Literature 'writing to the tune of *Rule Britannia*'. Thucydides, if I understood Cornford aright, 'wrote to the tune' of Aeschylus' *Agamemnon*. It was all there; only the catastrophe came in book vii at Syracuse—a book too soon; and Thucydides absentmindedly went on writing history 'as one who had lost his way', or something of that sort. If only other historians could lose their way as he did, telling of the Athenian revolution—a very odd judgment. But the first half of the book was more arguable. It was a commercial war, though Thucydides never had guessed it, as the German Julius Beloch had done some years ahead of Cornford. So much prelude. I fell in with Henry Jackson one day just outside the great gate of Trinity, and he gave me his judgment of Cornford's book—very briefly. And then he laughed. 'Did you hear Verrall's lecture on the *Birds*?' Of course I had. 'Then, don't you see? the war was hatched in that synagogue down in the Peiraieus!' This was an echo of Liberal talk about the Boer War. What Jackson himself thought of that talk, I don't know. I was a 'Colonial', and did not hold with the annexation of British territory by aggressive neighbours; and there I leave it. My mind is not changed on that subject, whatever is done with Newfoundland.

William Ridgeway was one of the great figures of that period —a great splendid, unchastened, belligerent Irishman, capable of warm friendship and of unhesitating animosity. Nobody would call him unprejudiced, and he could provoke the mildest and most tranquil people. But at an early stage, when it meant a great deal, he had let me know that he believed a bit in me; and I never forgot this. One had to remember it now and then. Thus, early

in the war of 1914, he met me and harangued me on the wicked
dissenters; if the Kaiser would only promise to destroy the
cathedrals on the conquest of England, the wicked dissenters
would welcome him with open arms. I didn't think so; but I had
been brought up not to contradict my seniors; so I listened to the
tale of dissenters and sin, till I got the chance of a side issue, and
asked him, not quite as innocently as it may have seemed, about
Cornford's book on Greek Comedy. It was my salvation.
Instantly the wicked dissenters and the Kaiser and the cathedrals
faded out of the picture; and the storm broke on the absent
Cornford. *Sic me servavit Apollo.*

One could not help being fond of the furious old man. I used
to meet him at the Classical board. His huge broad-brimmed
straw hat, broader of brim than any in Cambridge, always lay on
the table at the back of the room. When we were done, he would
collect it and take off his gown; and then it was my function to
get him down the stairs, which always frightened me a bit. He
told me that his wife and daughter could never quite foresee
what he would see or miss; and we never had an accident. But
one day I told him we were like Antigone and Oedipus. I was
Antigone, and Oedipus was a blind old man who was good at
cursing. Ridgeway laughed, and began reciting Sophocles, and
so through the streets to Caius. 'That was a very honest vote you
gave about so and so', he said to me, and I record his verdict with
pride. We skirted some disagreement when I was a candidate for
the Oratorship; he had a horrid suspicion that a wicked dissenter
would say something dreadful about the long string of generals
and admirals who were to be presented to us. But that was a lost
fear; and when he found his anticipations were wrong, he wrote
to me delightfully.

Perhaps the story I like best about Ridgeway was one I heard
some summers ago in a pleasant garden in a country place in
Ontario, which the reader will not have heard of—a few miles
west of Port Hope. It was Corelli who told me—the most
effectual administrator of the great Museum in Toronto. In his

youth Corelli had had a winter in Egypt with Flinders Petrie, and he visited Cambridge on his homeward way; and here he met Ridgeway. 'I hear ye've been in Egypt with Petrie?' Yes, he had. 'Then what do you think of these?' Ridgeway dived into his trouser pocket, where he was always liable to have some vital relic of the past that might clinch a theory. This time 'these' proved to be a handful of scarabs. Corelli took them and looked them over; 'I think', he said, 'they're all of them forgeries.' 'What makes ye think that, young man?' said Ridgeway; 'I can tell you some very good judges are against you.' 'Because', said Corelli, unabashed, 'they're all of them made of Labradorite; and that stone isn't found in Egypt.' 'Ye're quite right', said Ridgeway, delighted; 'I had them made myself, at the best lapidary's in Dublin; they've been most useful to me!'

I wish I could reproduce, in letters, the 'Hay! hay!' or 'heh! heh!' of Ridgeway, which came when he had pulled off an argument that seemed good—like Humpty Dumpty's 'There's glory for you'. It often came, but when he read his dissertation for the Greek professorship, after Henry Jackson's death, to the Council of the Senate, it seemed that by an effort he repressed the great ejaculation, till—well, he lectured on the trial scene on the shield of Achilles, and did it admirably; but at last one of his arguments was too good for further repression, and the paragraph ended with a joyous 'Hay! hay!' Why the Council didn't elect him, I don't know; I think they might better have done so, but perhaps they thought a neutral tint would be safer—a characteristic Cambridge view. 'Safety first' is a Cambridge watchword, not quite a heroic note. Thus

> 'I *think*', the Wrangler said, 'it's white;
> Still it's important to be right;
> So, while fresh evidence we lack,
> It might seem safer to say black.'

However, Ridgeway was subsequently knighted, and his portrait was painted for the hall of Caius—a portrait that partially represents him. He lived a long and joyous life of battle and theory, routing his wicked foes and reinforcing his theories with fresh evidence that always turned up. He took the chair once for a lecture of Gilbert Murray's to the Cambridge Classical Society. I have heard from Gilbert Murray perhaps the best lecture of my life on a Classical subject; but this one was (*salva reverentia*) not one of the best. It was about σπαραγμός; all Greek tragedy was to turn on the 'tearing up' of somebody or other in the process of it. It doesn't sound quite probable; but at least that lecture ended so. For Ridgeway moved a vote of thanks—all of us greatly indebted to Professor Murray for coming over, as he does, to lecture to us, and so on; and then suddenly a burst of controversy quite irresistible, and Murray and his lecture were 'torn up'—to shreds;— but that is not the real point, we are all so much indebted—and then a second eruption and the lecturer had more σπαραγμός—and Ridgeway made a third plunge at our gratitude and we all got away. He gave me a lift in the hansom that always took him back to Ditton; and, as we settled down, he ejaculated 'Damned rot'. This last Murray did not hear; but I have a pleasant recollection of his twinkle on one occasion when he recalled Ridgeway's 'vote of thanks'.

I have another recollection of that cab. Lady Ridgeway had been very ill; and he opened out to me about her; they had been friends since he was sixteen; and 'the best of it is, the old girl's better'. A later illness carried her off, and he did not long survive her, nor could one have wished that he should.

This chapter would not be complete if I did not at least mention James Adam. Of course it will not be complete anyhow—cannot be. But it would be unjust not to supplement matter incorporated in Mrs Adam's memoir of him. Adam, at an early date after my return from Canada, sought me out; and an intimacy grew up, which made amends for what I lost in leaving my colleagues in Canada. He used to bicycle with me—generally (as I used to say) with St Paul standing on the back-step of his wheel in his most Stoical mood. Adam talked incessantly of Stoicism, and it did one good to provoke him by suggesting that Stoicism was an admirable religion for a man who did not want a religion, and then to listen to the magnificent explosion that might follow. One day he brought one of his boys to ride with us, as he 'wanted him to see some really good cycling'. (He ought to have seen Rendel Harris on a free wheel coming full tilt down the Gogs.) Adam had a sort of cranberry flavour about his talk and his mind —sharp and satisfying and very attractive. I used to go across to his study after Sunday morning service. He sat on a sofa in the corner of it writing his Gifford lectures, which he would always talk over. He wore, on those summer days, indoors the most battered of old straw hats—'to keep his brains in', he said. Letters that he wrote me, vivid and characteristic, are in the memoir. His conscience used to smite him if, as he looked back, the cranberry flavour had been too strong; it never had. 'Don't go back to Canada; Pax vobiscum' followed one explosion.

Then one dreadful morning at Sheringham I saw his death announced in the London paper. Next day I had a letter from him to say there was to be an operation. The loss was unspeakable. So passed out of my life one of the happiest influences I have known in Cambridge.

Chapter IV

HIGH TABLE

In my first chapter I have looked back over the centuries of Cambridge. In my second and third I have tried to picture the men I found here—the men who were to educate me. I now turn to the High Table, which I reached in November 1892, and attempt a further series of portraits of men who were really older, most of them, than our lecturers.

I

Of the older generation who survived into our days, quite the oddest was Peter Hamnett Mason, the President of the College and lecturer in Hebrew. He had written a Hebrew grammar in the form of 'Letters to a Duchess'. Duchesses may now and then wish to learn Hebrew, like the retired Scottish grocer who thought it might be fitting for him to learn to address the Creator in His own language. Peter's duchess appears to have been imaginary, or at most (legend said) his cat. But there the book was, and he had enlisted the enthusiasm of his pupils. For when the Regius Professorship of Hebrew became vacant, and the electors, not quite unintelligibly, fought shy of the queer old man and elected a much less picturesque figure, a Trinity man, who held the post for many years, Peter's pupils rose in indignation, levied contributions on one another and themselves, and founded a University prize to perpetuate the old man's memory, the Mason Prize for Biblical Hebrew. Biblical—that was it, for Peter would have nothing to say to modern theories as to the language, and, playing on a technical point about the tenses, he refused any adherence to these 'Imperfect' scholars and maintained the allegiance of his youth to 'the grammarians of the Past and of the Future'. I heard it suggested that, if every copy of the Hebrew Bible were lost, Peter could reproduce the whole from memory.

Youth somehow can never conceive that old men were really
once-on-a-time young; and probably none of us supposed that
Peter could have been young. He saw imperfectly or supposed
he did; and, when you came to close quarters with him, raised his
spectacles to peer at you, and his welcome might be effusive.
Bushe-Fox, it was said, had to see him, and was welcomed as his
father's son—'I remember your father'. 'I don't think so, sir; my
father died long ago and was never in Cambridge.' 'Ah! then!
it was your elder brother.' But the relentless undergraduate had
no brother. 'Then it must have been yourself. How do you do,
Mr Bushe-Fox?' Bushey was eminent in the L.M.B.C. world;
and on one occasion Peter 'halled' the whole of the first boat.
They came simultaneously and sat on some forms in his outer
room, while one of them went in for the interview. He left the
door ajar, and argued their case so adroitly and the conversation
grew so ludicrous, that his friends outside were shaking with
laughter. Suddenly the door opened and out swept Peter; instantly every man hid his laughter in his hands. Peter saw a row
of men with their faces hidden and their backs shaking; he instantly grasped the situation, but misconceived it. He laid a
friendly hand on the nearest shoulder—'Come! come! this is not
manly', he said.

Heitland, whose comments were often caustic, declared that the
old man's elaborate and gesturing old-world politeness had no
relation with any old-world manners, but was his own absurd
invention; and it was certainly odd. He was a great walker;
walking was safe and reasonable in those days before motors; and
you would see Peter in academic dress stalking with great strides
along the Trumpington road, well in the carriage way, swinging
as he strode with arms flung out, and his College cap waved
abroad in his right hand. A wicked undergraduate would enjoy
disconcerting him by taking off his hat to him. But he was not,
or had not always been, as simple as he looked. Heitland maintained that the simplicity concealed a foxy cunning, and Herbert
Foxwell had a story of some undergraduate dashing to morning

chapel clad in little but a surplice; Peter recognized this impropriety, and with his old-world courtesy insisted at the end of the service on taking the man there and then from the chapel to his rooms for breakfast, and then without more ado sweeping him off for a long country walk. There seem, in retrospect, to be some difficulties in the story; a long country walk in a surplice was surely unusual; but that was the story and if you knew Peter Mason it was not too wildly improbable. He did great distances when he started. Legend also said that Peter had been proctor, and, finding a man carrying his gown, told him: 'I don't think that the gentleman, to whom you are carrying that gown, would like you to wear his cap.' His colleague, they said, was G. F. Browne, afterwards Bishop of Bristol. In those days undergraduates would fling coppers from the gallery. 'Do you know why?' Browne asked Mason; 'they are Peter's pence.' 'I had the idea', rejoined Peter, 'that they are sometimes called "browns".'

Peter as a member of the High Table was a constant source of interest. When the governing body met, and a vote had to be taken, he as President was always asked to vote first, and very commonly rejoined: 'I do not vote.' So regular was this that once, when after dinner we were asked to vote on a prize which William Bateson offered for the best joke on something, W. C. Summers captured everybody by saying in Peter's exact tones: 'I will vote, but I do not wish my vote to be *recorded*.' It was Peter's function to say Grace after dinner in hall, but he always passed the Grace-tablet to A. J. Stevens, who was another clerical from earlier days.

Stevens was an unfortunate man. A change of ecclesiastical allegiance permitted him to take orders in the Church of England, and in those days, provided he did not marry, he could hold his Fellowship for life, and he did hold it. It was said that he tried schoolmastering, at which it was obvious he could never have been a success; but he could fall back on his Fellowship. He invented, Foxwell said, a contrivance for lubricating railway engines and patented it; nothing came of it, till he let the patent lapse, and then it was widely adopted by the railway companies. So back to College he came, did a little examining, read the *Daily Mail*, dined in hall, spoke if you spoke to him, read Grace for Peter, and otherwise sank into nonentity. He did not read Grace well; *eructavit cor meum*, was the Biblical comment of the Rabelais scholar W. F. Smith; Barlow put it more gently—'We had several bubbles to-night.' It was curious how a man originally of some ability could be so content to be a cipher. One night Heitland, to tease the amiable J. T. Ward, remarked that there was reason to suppose that *Ally Sloper's Half Holiday*, a 'comic' picture-paper long ago defunct, was chiefly supported by the clergy of the Church of England—a wicked expansion of the alleged fact that C. E. Graves had a file of it from the start and had been awarded by Ally the order of F.O.S. (Friend of Sloper). Suddenly the voice of Stevens was heard from a place or two up the table: 'Ehm! some numbers of *Ally Sloper* are quite good.' Heitland, looking over his spectacles, settled the matter: 'So are many of the clergy!' And there it rested.

Once to the surprise of everybody Stevens rose in a College meeting and made a suggestion about the place for the War Memorial, but it was still-born. Once he printed a queer slip about the possibility of some text in the Gospel being right and intelligible, concluding, as it were with a sigh, that nowadays people were more apt to reject Scripture. He offered some quantities of this slip to the Dean, in case it might be of use to distribute among undergraduates. He lived to a considerable age, and expressed an odd regret about T. G. Bonney who died at ninety, bent but alive and pungent. Bonney, Stevens suggested, had permanently weakened his constitution by exposure on the Alps in his youth. Somehow one did not think of Bonney as prematurely enfeebled. Stevens long persevered with his afternoon walk to Hyde Park Corner, dragging more and more sadly.

PROFESSOR MAYOR

From the etching by H. von Herkomer

II

A far more notable figure than these two men was John E. B. Mayor, the professor of Latin, who succeeded Mason as President of the College. He read Grace himself, and his reading of it was remarkable for its clearness and dignity. He was an advocate of reading aloud as an aid to health and strength, and to this he added a fervent belief in vegetarianism. Rumour from the kitchen suggested he was not as entirely vegetarian as he supposed; those vegetable soups—'we couldn't let the old gentleman die on our hands'—were fortified more than he knew. Whether it was vegetarianism at the back of it or, as I have heard, philanthropy, the wish to start a protégé as a grocer, he took up with a project of making marmalade at one time. To economize, apparently, he used the jars of well-known makers and had a label of his own pasted over their embossed name; and before long he had the law upon him, and had to make some sort of public apology; and that was the end of his venture. But he continued to repudiate flesh-food; the days were past when he was 'a sepulchre for fowl'.

When A. E. Housman, who succeeded him in the Latin Chair, declared in his inaugural address that Mayor 'sternly limited himself' to what interested him, his words struck oddly upon College people. There was nothing very stern about it and very little limitation; the old man wandered as he pleased; preached sermons in the College chapel (and printed them in whole or in part[1]) on Spanish Protestants; denounced the trifling mind and manners of the young; annotated in huge folios the deaths, births and marriages and so forth of members of the College; indulged that fancy for making notes that besets aged scholars, with Lewis and Short's Latin dictionary as a foundation. 'Impudent fellows,' he called Lewis and Short; 'when they say a word is rare, I write *not* in the margin; why, they dare to say that *adjutorium* is rare; from Theodore Priscian alone I have gleaned 740 instances.'

[1] One of his sermons ends at the foot of the page in the middle of a sentence that was to be completed in another quire, and never was.

Youth was often so degenerate. That young Oxford man who was reported to have said that he 'did not mind going to college chapel; he rather liked it'—'verily', declaimed Mayor (and he printed it, too), 'Oxford churchmanship must be near extinction, if this puss young gentleman be a type of it.' At Cambridge there were other signs of intellectual poverty; many of the football men, he had reason to believe, 'had libraries of less than 2000 books'. This last was true, whatever was the state of Oxford churchmanship. And one recalls his resolution to have no mercy on ignorance 'significant and budge'.

At one stage a terrible misfortune befel him. The copy of Lewis and Short, in which he was registering his reading and his corrections of their 'impudence', disappeared, and could not be found. It seemed only too likely that it had been stolen—what a thesaurus of learning it would afford to a rival scholar, who might wish to supersede Lewis and Short—a German, perhaps. That Mayor would concentrate long enough to supersede them himself with a work of his own, nobody who knew him would have believed; but making notes toward a project was another thing, an enjoyable task that gave the sensation of valuable work. But the book was gone—stolen! Mayor notified the learned journals and all who read them, scholars and booksellers, that if they were offered this lost dictionary, they must know it was stolen from him. But it was not stolen, nor indeed very far away. His bedmaker, innocent soul, had used it—not to produce a rival lexicon, but to support a chest of drawers which had lost a foot. *Notumque fovens quid femina possit.*

I once attended a course of his lectures. His subject was Tertullian, whom I was then reading. He took the *Apology*, translated a chapter or two rapidly, and then dictated a series of references, taking word after word and telling us in what authors (with chapter and verse) these words occurred. It had very little bearing on the mind or character or theology of Tertullian. But the other man, attending the lectures, shared Mayor's passion for lexicography, and faithfully took the references down, and when

Mayor died, he produced for Mayor's brother, Joseph, and from Mayor's notes, all that mass of erudition, with which were printed his own translation and Oehler's text. I still think that it all tells you very little that will make you realize or understand Tertullian; but Professor Souter of Aberdeen stands in the front rank of British scholars. He was the industrious apprentice; I was the idle one. *Hinc illae lacrimae.*

Mayor, for all his declamations and denunciations of 'impudent' dictionary-makers and idle youth and trivial modern writers of books, was a kind old man. An early walk in the courts might bring you in contact with him as he left the chapel; and nothing would do but he would take you up to his rooms over the Shrewsbury gate, and there, undaunted by cold, and forgetful of food (yours and his) he would discourse to you at length of matters scholarly or Spanish, splendidly irrelevant, and give you at the end some volume of value or interest from the point of view of pure learning, but it again might not be—probably never was—very relevant to you or your work. But that did not matter—nor cold nor appetite for breakfast; you had been listening to a great scholar and bore away for ever the picture of the gleaming, bright, kind eyes. They look at you still from Herkomer's portrait. The portrait of Mason by C. E. Brock, now relegated to a lecture-room, was not so generally esteemed as a picture, but nothing could have given you a truer conception of Peter Mason, 'still life' as it was.

III

A far more significant man than any of them was George Downing Liveing. Mayor as a professor was virtually useless to students or to the College; except as a lovable, discursive, irrelevant survival of the past. Nobody adopted his vegetarianism, nobody was much concerned with his Spanish Protestants, and in those days nobody cared about the lexicography of Latin authors between A.D. 300 and 700. He read well in chapel, and it was always interesting to hear now and then about *adjutorium*, or the foolish luxury of the age; of course, people liked him as 'a dear old thing', but he was not really a factor in anybody's affairs. Liveing had been neck-deep in University business all his life, maker of a department, builder of a laboratory, acute, incisive, practical. The legend survived of his hot temper, which taken with his red hair (we were told it had been red), won him the nickname of 'the Red Precipitate'. He was a chemist, but he was much else—a man of wide travel in the age before all dons went round or about the world, a man of experience and judgment, courteous, quiet and shrewd.

He had been in Italy in the stirring Garibaldi days, and, as an Englishman, had seemed to Italians a natural ally, but it was characteristic of him perhaps that he stood aloof and would not burn his fingers in other people's quarrels. Of late years we have seen an immense deal in Cambridge of enthusiasm for foreign adventure, but there was nothing Quixotic about Liveing; a wind-mill was a windmill to him and he did not meddle with it. 'A poor spirit?' Not at all, he served his own generation and he served them well, high-minded, broad in survey, disinterested and active. Once he astonished us rather uncomfortably; he told an American visitor in hall that he had been in America 'just before the war'. We knew he had not; he was over eighty, and was still living in his house next door to Newnham College, 'The Pightle'. Could the old man be suddenly struck in some way, and wandering in mind? Not he! His next sentence was 'Buchanan was president then and people were saying that if Lincoln were elected there would be civil war'. So it was the American Civil War that was in his mind, brought back by the visitor.

In those early days he had tasks we little expected. One night in the Combination Room talk drifted to Paley's *Evidences*, and some one broached the subject to Liveing, who sat near, silent and a little deaf. For a moment his face looked rather blank, and then it lit up all over, in a way familiar to us and very pleasant. And he spoke. 'I lectured on Paley in college for two years', he said; and he a chemist! These were the days when people spoke reverentially of the fallen Asquith as 'one of the elder statesmen'. And Liveing went on to say that among his pupils had been Asquith's Head-master—Edwin Abbott. He was indeed very old. I have always felt that I never witnessed so magnificent a snub administered as he gave to an aged Johnian one Sunday morning in the court. J. M. Wilson, who in ages past had been Headmaster of Clifton and was now Canon of Worcester, had come up to preach a University sermon at the age of eighty-seven. The two men had been at morning service in the College chapel, and, coming out, Wilson went up to Liveing and said: 'I think we were con-temporaries.' 'No,' said Liveing, severely, 'I am nine years senior to you.' We all hoped he would reach one hundred; but a year after the encounter with J. M. Wilson, stepping back to avoid a car, he upset a girl on a bicycle, and fell himself; his thigh was broken, irrecoverably; he lingered a few months, and died at ninety-seven. 'No,' he said to me, 'she was not to blame.'

He founded, I think, some of the choral studentships; but it was kept very dark where they came from. I used to sit nearly oppo-site him at the College Council, and the grave quiet figure remains before my mind. He took very little part in discussion; he even seemed aloof from it, as if he did not hear or greatly care to hear; but he followed what was going on, and when the moment came for voting, he voted at once, without any of Peter Mason's atti-tudes, voted straight and for the fundamentally sensible view of the matter in hand. The University presented a Latin address to him on the completion of seventy-five years of continual residence without a gap of a term from his matriculation. Someone had suggested it should be in English, but the shrewder judgment prevailed that Liveing would prefer it in Latin. He asked to see it, however, before the meeting in the Combination Room at which the Vice-Chancellor presented it. He replied in English in a speech of quiet dignity and retrospect; and everybody was pleased that the address had been made.

Liveing's portrait by Sir George Reid is one of the happiest (and one of the noblest) that we have. He was already an old man when it was painted, and he lived another quarter of a century. He and Reiḍ 'tumbled to one another'; he did not use that phrase —of course not! it was not the vocabulary of his day or of his mind; but that was what happened. They suited one another, and as you look at the portrait you do not need to be told so; Reid caught the very Liveing that we knew and lived with—his dignity, his very masculine grace, his grave kindliness, his splendid old age. The portrait has only to be contrasted with Sir George Reid's picture of Sir Richard Jebb, done for Trinity College, and one sees how Liveing captured his painter and was at ease with him.

Liveing was succeeded as President by Sikes.

IV

Robert Forsyth Scott was (like most Scotsmen) a son of the manse, and the manse was that of Dairsie in Fifeshire, where his father was the Church of Scotland minister. His mother, the daughter of Robert Forsyth, advocate, was in her later years a not unfamiliar figure in the courts of St John's, quietly making her way to the Bursary in I New Court, where her son sat under the portraits of the family. In Scotland it was more usual for the elder son to be called from the paternal side; here it was reversed, and George Scott was the younger son. The dedication of his well-known book, *The Burman, his life and notions, by Shway Yoe*, pictures the mother:

'When anything surprises or pleases a Burman, he never fails to cry out, Amè—mother. Following the national example, to whom can I better dedicate this book than to you, my dear Mother? Who else will be so eager to praise; so tender to chide, so soft to soothe and console; so prompt to shield and defend...?'

R. F. Scott was not an emotional man, most people would have said; but those about him, when in advanced old age his mother was taken from him, knew better, if he did not unpack his heart

PROFESSOR LIVEING
From the painting by Sir George Reid

with words. There, as in many other ways, he showed his race. With his brother he was always in close relations. George Scott did not make a brilliant start, but a job was found for him in a Burmese missionary school, and from it he passed to the press, to frontier delimitation, authorship and a knighthood. In those days of the press, R. F. Scott week by week sent him a 'London letter' for his paper; and 'you realize the immensity of space, my boy', he would say, 'when you have to fill four columns every week'. Scott was at the bar in those days.

To return to his own story and to get it in order, he had some schooling with his brother in Germany; and he used to tell of fights with German boys, repeated till he realized that 'Nicht wahr?' implied no doubt as to his veracity. In October 1871 he entered at St John's, where he became fourth Wrangler, a Fellow, and rowed in the third L.M.B.C. boat. He confessed to tears when he was turned out of the first boat—and to a vigorous undergraduate life with his lifelong friend, Sir Charles Parsons, the inventor of the turbine. For some time he taught at Christ's Hospital; and later on he used to examine there, as his friends remember. For when an Income Tax official inquired why, after three years, he omitted to enter any examining fees from that school, he wrote back that 'there is no accounting for the eccentricities of headmasters', which appears to have been understood even by a Government official.

In 1883 he came back to St John's as Bursar, and was soon to find enough to do. There was a familiar legend of his predecessor —that 'Betsey' Rayner, the hero of so many legends—striding in silence beside the farmer over a College farm, and at last inquiring, with his famous intonation: 'Mr Blank, do you find the cultivation of thistles remunerative?' Another style of pleasantry was needed, when the agricultural depression began in earnest in the late 'eighties; and Scott was equal to it. Everything that kindness and geniality and devotion to the College could do, he did. And he enjoyed any gleam of absurdity or nonsense that came. In those days (till 1906) letters were delivered round among the

College rooms by the postman; and Scott used to tell of the triumphant air with which a young postman (who rose high at the post office) laid on his table an envelope from one of his farmers, with the words 'There's no doubt who that is meant for'; and the address Scott saw was to 'the Senior Boozer'. He lamented humorously the hospitality he suffered in the farms, the dear people *always* cooking chickens for him, while he longed for beef. (Lunch in the Bursary was bread and jam.) Meanwhile, by taking the biggest venture of his bursarial life, he began to pull things straight for the College (which saw Fellowships fall to £80), by co-operating in the transformation of an impossible farm into the Sunningdale golf links, with an array of pleasant and expensive houses round them on College land.

One feature of his work was his tolerance of interruption. Few men had more work or more difficult; but, if you invaded the Bursary, you would see him look up over his glasses, and lay down his pen, with an air of relief, as if he were sick of solitude and wanted nothing more than a half-hour's crack. And let us supplement this with some words from the preface of the *Dictionary of National Biography* (which pleased him, as they well might): 'No inquiry addressed to Mr R. F. Scott, bursar of St John's College, Cambridge...has failed to procure a useful reply.' He had, he would say in later years, 'a passion for minute biography'. At one of the *D.N.B.* dinners, Mr Archbold says, he explained: 'I am here as an original authority.' The College *Eagle* celebrated this aspect of the Bursar as he then was:

> You may die in Oklahoma,
> Torres Straits, Tibet or Boma,
> You may bet your bottom dollar that you never will be missed;
> But, before a week has flitted,
> You will find yourself outwitted
> And your life and labours noted by Our Own Obituarist.

There were other verses, and the thing pleased Scott, who, in addressing himself to the writer of them, used 'O.O.O.' for his signature.

He was Proctor, too. A Proctor (said Foakes Jackson) who comes through without some loss of reputation does well. Scott gained regard by it; he was so human. He would tell tales of his Proctor days, beginning: 'When I was Proggins.' It was of him that a guilty Trinity man, now one of His Majesty's Judges, inquired: 'And where *is* St John's?' One night he entertained the University Boat (or L.M.B.C. I, it may have been), tendering them cigars as they left, with the friendly words: 'You will find my colleague at the gate.' The colleague was Neville of Sidney. They had duties to do, of which modern Proctors are happily relieved. Witness Scott's tale of his sufferings, when a young woman was arrested by him on a Sunday afternoon in the Backs, and sat down promptly under a tree, refusing to go to the Spinning House except in a cab, which the ass of a bulldog went (on foot) to the Railway Station to find, while a sympathetic crowd gathered round the sitting victim and her embarrassed captor. He used to tell, too, of a list of 'Persons Not Generally Known' published in *The Granta*, which included 'The Author of *The Theory of Determinants*'; and of the luckless undergraduate who tried to pay his six and eightpence in threepenny bits ('My savings, sir') and was told that it was not 'proctorial tender' even if it was (as he pleaded) 'legal tender'. There was a rider to that story. Scott demanded a pound, and told him to take his threepences; and 'How much have I fined you?' 'Thirteen and fourpence, sir.' '*I* knew,' added Scott; 'for there was a sovereign on the table, where there had been nothing before.'

An observation that he made about the College chapel is very characteristic. The great West window was the gift of undergraduates, and it pictures the Last Judgment. On the left hand of the Judge are the damned, and in the lowest left-hand corner the worst of them are already in very realistic flames. The authorities of the day had wished to signalize the undergraduate gift, and they recorded it on the window in Latin, but so placed that, as Scott pointed out, immediately below the souls in hell were the words JUNIORES COLLEGII ALUMNI.

He was a Major in the Volunteers of those times, and took part duly in their field days. He piloted new scholars and Fellows to the Lodge for the awful ceremony of admission. To a new Fellow who wondered if it was quite right for him to come punctually to hall and sit among his seniors, 'it might improve your mind', said Scott. He delved unceasingly into the College archives, and term by term *The Eagle* opened with 'Notes from the College Records'. He liked to quote a grumbling subscriber (in arrears, perhaps): 'Is good old Scott still doing those Notes? He must be a long way into futurity by now.' Scott was deeply conversant with the history, ancient and recent, of the College—so much so that it was said that business on the College Council always followed the same lines. The Master (Scott himself by now) said: 'Well, it was this way. In 1871...' (or whatever the date was). Sir Joseph Larmor would at once rejoin: 'It's the first I've heard of it.' H. F. Baker was apt to suggest: 'Couldn't we adjourn it till next week?' And Dr L. E. Shore, the Junior Bursar, said: 'Leave it to me.' (How one would like to digress on that last appeal!) Scott had other activities—on the Town Council, the Council of the Senate, the Conservators of the Cam, and the Conservative Association; but they did not interfere with his services to his friends and his leisure for them.

In 1908 he succeeded Dr Charles Taylor as Master. On the night of his election, he ended his speech to the Fellows with the hint that people say 'moss gathers in Lodges', and hoping that, if it did, they might remember it covered the remains of a good fellow. He was in due course Vice-Chancellor, and received the honorary degree of LL.D. at St Andrews, became a Bencher of Lincoln's Inn and was knighted in 1924. 'It was lucky Baldwin did it before he went out,' he said, 'for Ramsay might not have thought of it.' Everybody enjoyed the short speeches in which he would propose the health of new Fellows at the election feasts and he grew better and better at it. His ambition in his later years was to last out till he had served a full half-century as Bursar and Master; and his hope was fulfilled.

As one looks back upon the many years, one sees a figure always genial, always ready with some amusing story, always sympathetic with normal youth (less so with premature apostles or prigs of any age), always open-eyed for service to the College, devotion to which was the very core of his life and character.

V

Donald MacAlister was one of the ablest men in Cambridge two generations ago, and he was a Highlander. He came to St John's from a school in Liverpool; but he had been born in Scotland, and had the earlier part of his schooling there. The Scot in England, according to R. L. Stevenson, is always a foreigner. It is true; the Tweed is one of the broadest rivers of the world. Still more is the Highlander a stranger among Saxons; his mind works in a different way from theirs—works when theirs does not work, and has a sensitiveness quite unfamiliar; and all the traditions are different—different as the religion and the history of the two countries. The Saxon was perplexed by MacAlister, and was made uneasy by his uncanny cleverness, by the ease with which he did things and by the range of his knowledge and his capacity. In those days there was comparatively little first-hand acquaintance with the larger world; men went to Germany and Switzerland. MacAlister knew America and Canada. He thought once of going to McGill—would have gone, had not a great happiness moored him on this side. He was a medical man; but, incidentally he had been Senior Wrangler. Now it is not always realized to-day how serious a matter it was to be Senior Wrangler. There were men who could tell you the series of Senior Wranglers, dating them like Derby winners; the year was known by the Senior. Some Senior Wranglers never did anything at all, after achieving the degree; it was their high-water mark. With MacAlister, one felt it was a mere episode in a career that went far beyond it.

He handled University and College business with a quickness that shocked people. The type is familiar that never can make up its mind, that wants things postponed, and decides at last on a side issue. MacAlister would strike to the centre of the matter in hand, and strike to it quickly; and it took away the breath of the types just described; it seemed improper, too like levity. What other men laboured at, he seemed to do with a light touch; it was a burden to them to be accurate; he came naturally by it, and just did the thing, and went on unstaggered to the next. He had a ready pen, and could draft a resolution as readily as he seized the issue. He looked further afield than many of the men he had to work with; he had seen more, and he had realized more; and the local tradition meant less to him than the newer and larger idea. So, in the end he lost his seat on the Council of the Senate to a safe man (a very pleasant one) whose mental processes men could more easily foresee, and who abode with us for all his genial life. Not long afterwards MacAlister was called away from Cambridge to responsibilities of far more moment. Cambridge sometimes has rivalled Montezuma in the sacrifice of life on the altar of Safety.

Lady MacAlister has a delightful tale of his childhood. MacAlisters and Campbells had long fought for some castle in Cantyre, and after various alternations the Campbells secured it for ever in Queen Anne's reign. The small boy Donald was taken to see his grandfather MacAlister, and stood between the old man's knees. The old man made the child lift his hand to heaven and promise never to marry a Campbell—'there's crows and Campbells everywhere' he said. 'Will I tell you the three curses of Argyllshire?' said an old and rather bibulous wayfarer to a friend of mine who gave him a lift—'there's bracken, and there's rabbits, and there's Campbells'. Yet it was a Campbell prime minister who sent Donald to his main life-work, in Glasgow.

In the Principalship of Glasgow University he had (it might have been expected) a task to absorb all the energies that even he could bring to it. He was an amazing contrast to his predecessor, a tremendous divine of an oldish type. He threw himself into his work, including in it the civic life of the great city (very different from that of Cambridge), made himself a place among the men who counted most in one of the most living and active centres of the Empire, and enlisted them in the service of their University. Some twenty chairs or lectureships were added in his time. This in itself was no mean testimony to his gifts of insight, of organization and conciliation. And the city honoured him among her first men and magistrates. When at last he resigned his post, it chanced that another shortly fell vacant; and he succeeded Lord Rosebery as Chancellor of Glasgow University—unopposed—a remarkable tribute to a life's work, and one with friendship in it.

But in fact the University was not his whole life-work, and did not absorb all his energies. He was President of the General Medical Council for years; and the work of the Council (which would appear to outsiders to be sufficiently heavy) was sandwiched between days in the University. The nights he spent on the train.

In December 1913 he very nearly died of a haemorrhage from the stomach. A week or two later I saw him—propped up with pillows in his bed, rather bloodless, but cheerful and debonair as ever. Forty years and more of friendship always show the same picture—the friendly, smiling figure, never over-strained, never at a loss, always ready to do the kind thing that materially helped, and always quick to divine what it should be—the sort of friend that surmounts difficulties for you and makes life easier and more delightful. He recovered from his illness; and though never too strong (he picked up too much rheumatism in his ground-floor rooms in St John's), he lived to do another twenty years (or near it) of effective work.

He had a curious aptitude for learning languages—perhaps not up to Tripos standards; but he was not a Tripos candidate or examiner, and he could enjoy the languages as he went from one to another. The little book of *Echoes*, in which he published versions of poems from quite a number of languages, bears witness to this. It was not great poetry perhaps; he never suggested that; but his rendering in good Scots, in 'Lallan', of the lines Catullus wrote on the sparrow is perhaps the most charming ever made. Compare it, for instance, with the conscientious prose of the Eton master in the Loeb Library! Romany was one of his tongues. A gipsy woman appeared in Addenbrooke's, and he tried it on her; she 'didn't understand'; so he felt her pulse and did one or two things; and then, suddenly and offhand, in Romany: 'Open your mouth'; she opened it, and he laughed, and perhaps she did, too.

He had a stroke at last, with some loss of power on one side, but not on top. He was not 'dying atop', like Swift; there he lived to the end, weak in body, but clear in mind, with the old smile, and the familiar quick flash in the eyes. The end was not long, and he was released. I do not here speak of his Liberalism, his loyalty to the Presbyterian church of his fathers, his great public service, his many honours. I would rather close on a note of gratitude that he was of the same time and that I knew him so long and so well.

VI

Edward Ernest Sikes—

> Dust thou art, to dust returnest
> Was not spoke to Edward Ernest—

came to St John's from Aldenham, of which school he later on became a Governor. He was senior Classical scholar among undergraduates, and in his third year, when I came up, and my first impression of him was from behind—at the lectures of Haskins. As I write I can see Haskins grinning all over, having obviously caught Sikes's eye; for Haskins was human and a friend, as I have said in a previous chapter.

After that I did not see much of him, back or front, for some time. He did Archaeology for the Second Part of the Tripos, and he went out to Greece and there grew a beard, if I remember, but it may have been a friend. It did not, I think, reach England, but was commemorated by Theocritus; as Sikes told me:

οἴμοι τοῦ πώγωνος ὃν ἠλιθίως ἀνέφυσα.

After his Second Part he went to Winchester and taught for a term or two. The rest of his life was spent at Cambridge but for a semester (or words to that effect) at Harvard. He became a Fellow of the College in 1891, a lecturer shortly after, and about the end of the century, tutor. Lecturers are too obscure to achieve nicknames, but on becoming tutor he was christened. There was an early Victorian novelist, still read occasionally at that period, who had a character called Sikes; so the tutor inherited his Christian name and was long known as Billy. Apart from the surname there was little in common between the characters. In old age he was given a more affectionate, a more paternal, prefix. Now that I speak of old age, let me add a word on his magnificent and enviable head of white hair, which, however, he seemed not to like. When his white hair grew long, it would turn a little yellow at the end; and when a colleague in some doggerel suggested that it proved the saffron rams of Virgil, he replied with some Latin elegiacs, ending

Mox mihi canities concolor adveniet.

In those early years he had his brother A. A. Sykes (with a 'y') about in Cambridge—a Russian scholar and translator of Gogol, a genial humourist, a 'Cantabard' and 'Universifier' in *The Granta*, and a contributor to *Punch*.

As Junior Fellows, and both of us Classical (I was elected in November 1892), Sikes and I were rather thrown together—not reluctantly. We began doing compositions together—generally in Greek verse—some of which I have had till quite lately. We walked together—I do not mean what Peter Green in those times called 'soul-destroying walks', but reasonable distances—and the memory stays with me of one towards Girton village, when we capped Browning quotations, Sikes carrying (you would not

7-2

believe it) an improvised flag. Once we went to the seaside together and were blessed with sunshine, Fairlight Glen-way. Then
a big separation. In 1896 I went to Canada, with no expectation
of return. But the College recalled me, and the day after I landed
in England, in 1901, I met Sikes by the big archway of the New
Court cloister—an illuminating encounter. He was tutor, as I
said; and I learnt then, though I did not realize how universal it
was, that you never speak to a tutor whose mind is quite dis-
engaged. I also learnt that my vocabulary needed to be Euro-
peanized. We greeted, spoke a few words, and then, 'Excuse me',
said Sikes, and turned to speak to a young man. He came back
to me. 'Was that a student?' I asked simply. 'We don't use that
word here', said Sikes austerely. We always used it in Canada;
but I learnt my lesson, and the word has been for forty years
strange to my lips, never at any rate applied to a member of this
College.

Nearly forty years—and we both gave lectures, and we wrote
books and read each other's MSS. and proofs. Of course I never
heard a lecture of his, but I heard about them. There was no 'erm-
nerm-ner'; everything was written, everything was read. 'Do
you know those red text-books of Macmillan's?' a man said to
me, 'well, Sikes's lectures could be printed as they stand to be one
of them.' I think this was a pity. Sikes evidently did not trust
himself as an extempore lecturer; perhaps memories of Haskins
swung him to the opposite extreme. All along he showed a
curious mixture of certainty and distrust; he had no doubt about
his opinions, but he had little adventure in his make-up. I recall
a case (I must not be too explicit) where we differed about a man;
I had a much higher opinion of him than Sikes had, and I got my
way—and found that Sikes was right. There was no recrimination,
but it was made clear that I had to mop up the spill I had made.
There was one fine characteristic about Sikes, which not everybody *could* know. Over those many years various appointments
were made in College. Nobody gets his way all the time, and
Sikes did not; but, the appointment once made, the man was

Sikes's colleague, and he must have been good at guessing if he realized that he had not been Sikes's choice. He could work with people he did not want, and do it in such a way that they would not readily guess his initial views. Some part of this grace (that is what it was) may have been due to a profound loyalty to the College. Few living to-day can have any idea what the College owes to the loyal service of Tanner and Sikes; Tanner was naturally, as senior man, and because he was built that way, more in the foreground; he had easier ways of intercourse; but there was always there the steady, dogged loyalty of Sikes co-operating —dogged, yes, and almost dour sometimes.

His early interest in archaeology led him to the Homeric Hymns, which he edited with Mr T. W. Allen of Oxford (1904). Allen was a literalist, an adherent of 'the MS.'; 'the kind of man', said Sikes to me one day, 'who would print ἀπό with the accusative, because it was in the MS., and would write a note to say it was a rare usage'. It was a good book; it has been long out of print, and it has been re-edited by Mr Halliday; but I am not clear that the immense additions of general learning, with which the new edition bulges, really make it a much better book. There is a feeling among some scholars that no variety of literature can be good except the encyclopaedic. Now Sikes had had a turn for modelling in clay—and for writing Greek iambics and Latin hexameters—and in both fields he had developed a sense of form. His next two books, on Greek and on Roman poetry, were not encyclopaedias, they were books, real books. They embodied ideas; and that of course limits a man and limits a book; they were to suggest and to quicken. The one I liked best was on Roman poetry; and a small thing will show how the book appealed to others. A favourite sort of question in the English Tripos was to quote a sentence, aphorism, idea or something of the kind, and invite the candidates to say what they thought of it. In the spring after Sikes's *Roman Poetry* appeared, the chairman of the examiners had to tell his colleagues, that, with no disrespect to the book or its author, he thought *three* quotations from one book rather many for *one* Tripos. Professor Souter of Aberdeen had a great admiration for the book and set it to be read by his students (perhaps the word may be used of Scots). Sikes used to read MSS. of mine, and in particular 'fair copies' and drafts of my Latin speeches. He was a most invaluable critic; 'he stuck his finger on the place, and said Thou ailest here and here'—very definite he was and very liable to be right. Where we differed was on English verse, where I was thoroughly conservative, and found him painfully *libre*; but I never could budge him.

Take all in all, his scholarship, his turn for ideas and form, his interest in science (he wrote a book on Lucretius too), you might say that, but for his shyness, he might have made a far bigger figure than he did; he had the gifts for it.

When Professor Liveing died, after his accident at ninety-seven, it was generally agreed that Sikes was the man to succeed him as President of the College. It involved some publicity, which was not acceptable. He mastered the after-dinner Grace with a little rearrangement of the Latin at the end; and, though the Professor of Latin—it was Housman—told him maliciously that he had 'heard Mayor read it', most of us liked Sikes's rendering of it, unless perhaps a Classical man or a stray conservative preferred *omnibus Christianis*. The illnesses of Scott threw work and responsibility and publicity on Sikes, culminating in the dinner to honorary graduates in 1933, when Sikes presided most happily and a pleasant speech was given by the genial Earl of Athlone and an amazingly interesting one by W. B. Yeats on lines of his own —very fresh and alive about Poetry and not about the merits of the graduates or the honour done them.

Sikes was happy in this, that serious illness did not come till the very end of his career, hardly anything of the kind in the many years of work. His life was given to the College, and he did little outside. His short period at Harvard seems to have been uneasy —perhaps dyspeptic in the main; to live in lodgings in America and 'eat' elsewhere is rough work; but his style of lecturing may have been above the men he had to teach, implying a great deal sounder training in Classics than most of them had had. He never liked inaccuracy; he complained of it in a bishop; but he once came near a public exhibition of it himself. In his earlier days he was Librarian of the Union Society, and it fell to him to read in public the list of books given to the Union Library with the giver indicated in each case; and it appeared on the surface that he wanted us to believe 'the book Genesis' was given to us 'by the author'. Such benevolence on the part of Moses startled his listeners for the moment; there was an explanation, it was a less interesting donor, and it came out that Sikes was accurate again.

A genuine scholar—shy, even timid, as a good many scholars are—careful and conscientious, reserved, thoroughly English— no other country could have produced him—a reliable and loyal colleague, he served the College and the cause of Classics well. It might be hard to say which meant more to him, but in serving one he served both.

Chapter V

CHANGES

I

It was a quip of my Father's long ago that the authentic words of Adam to Eve as they left Paradise were: 'My dear, we live in times of transition.' It is nowadays, I believe, attributed to Dean Inge; perhaps he thinks he coined it; perhaps he did, for great sayings are repeated again and again. Aelius Donatus, the grammarian quoted by St Jerome, put the thing once and for all (and many others must have echoed it from their hearts): *Pereant qui ante nos nostra dixerunt.* Whoever spoke first about times of transition, the years since I first knew Cambridge deserve that description. Within my lifetime, a few years (as I would now reckon them) before I came into residence, the doors were opened to dissenters, freedom was given to Fellows of Colleges to marry, the taking of holy orders was no longer required. All these changes rested on definite enactments, Royal Commission, Parliament and so forth. There were other changes devised by the University itself, and carried out by 'Graces' of the Senate; and still a third type of change that came neither from Act of Parliament nor Grace of the Senate, but in response to changing habits in the country at large, changes in social ways, political ideas, standards of education, theological conceptions and the decay of sentiment for 'organized religion'. Such things as the motor-car, cheaper and easier foreign travel, the gramophone, the wireless, modify our outlooks more than we suppose. 'The unimaginable touch of Time', if you prefer to put it poetically and to avoid detail. New sciences have arisen, clamours for new subjects of study, new conceptions of education, vocational training being one of them—and perhaps a lapse from the ideal of training the mind to that of storing the memory. Simultaneously we are confronted with the idea that the main function of a University is to examine and to assess a man's powers of memory and his adroitness in baulking an examiner's quirks, and then to tie a label to him and send him out to govern England or some parts of the Empire, to control little boys, to manage a parish, to conduct a business and so forth. Exactly; there we touch the services a citizen renders to his country; and one may wonder whether we have trained the citizen for any real kind of task, or whether our notion of packing his memory with dead information and then emptying it over an examination paper is any kind of training at all. The training of young men was discussed by Plato and his friends—and probably long before them, ever since two men aged forty wondered what to do with their sons aged sixteen; and probably in every age there has been disagreement, some standing for all old ways and no change, others for all possible 'reforms' and no old ways, and a good many dissatisfied with both attitudes, conscious of difficulties in changing situation and conscious that a younger generation is rightly or wrongly impatient.

II

Changes in the University, then; and first of all marriage. It came in first in 1882, when, as J. R. Tanner told me, 'there was a great rush to the altar'. Marriage alters many things. A legendary senior of some College, so they told us in my youth, was asked what he thought of it, and, after some slight reflexion, he said: 'The breakfasts are better, but the dinners are not nearly so good.' Few men, when they marry, realize the immensely practical nature of woman; 'you are so *concrete*', said a man of my acquaintance to his sister-in-law. You will find the adjective in one of the letters of the Carlyles, applied to the woman. Lord Salisbury himself was criticized, they say, by his wife: 'he may understand how to govern the empire, but he is not fit to be left

in charge of children.' 'We are, all of us, bad fathers', said a
Cambridge philosopher to me. Perhaps it will not seem a
superfluous tangent to what we have in hand, to remind a reader
of the economic aspects of University life, which, as we noticed,
were observed from the first arrival here of students, who were
celibate. Wife, house, children, their food, clothing and education, mean problems those students never knew—to say nothing
of the horrid levies that town authorities and landlords make.
We have to remember the bearing of all this on College finance.
Are you going to raise your lecturer's stipend so high as to permit
him to educate his children, or will it be for the benefit of the
College to let him go to a better paid post (say) in a new University and to replace him with somebody cheaper? I have known
of a Mathematician being deliberately sacked from a New Zealand
University not on account of inefficiency or bad character, but
avowedly because the governing body calculated on getting a
younger man at a cheaper rate. And what becomes of education,
when School or College or University 'economizes' in that way?
What is £50 a year saved, if it means a real teacher lost and re-
placed by a good examinee with a paper record, and if, as it will,
it gives administrators a precedent and the College (or University)
a bad name?

But marriage in Cambridge has made other problems. No
doubt there is something in what women say—that it is good for
a man that he should be married. There is something like that in
an early chapter of Genesis. No doubt—at least when one reads
old Gunning, and recalls the stories that survive from a century
or a century and a half ago, one realizes that stricter canons of
moral conduct have prevailed since 1882, perhaps still prevail.
That is something to credit to the reform. But there is another
thing. Some time ago a newcomer to Cambridge, a man of high
place and distinction, told me that he found us much more alike
than he expected. There is a saying of President Taft that is quoted
and deserves to be studied: 'Men', he said, 'are different, but
husbands are all the same.' Yes, and a flippant jingle embodies

what he said, with a slight development that might be considered
too:

> Because he was different from other men
> In mind and manners and frame,
> She married the man; and then she began
> To try to make him the same.

It is not *all* of it the woman's intention or her endeavour; the
great similarity of domestic conditions works for it—children,
servants, drains, doctor's bills, noise, worry; it is the same sub-
stantially everywhere. Similar conditions produce similar results;
and everything in Cambridge tends to grade us. What may be
missing in the domestic circle, is supplied by the headmaster or
the headmistress. It may be a good thing to have wives and
children, cooks and schoolmistresses, rubbing off all our corners.
A parable does not always help; you can't make a road with
round pebbles. It is well that our pupils see in their lecturers men
disciplined by the normal life of a good citizen; but again the
lecturer may be in such economic bondage—with extra work,
examining and so on—that his intellectual life receives no new
stimulus, that he gains no new vision in his studies, that he becomes a sort of gramophone record, that in fact Mr A. D. Godley
of Oxford was too near the mark when he wrote of College
lectures:

> And listening crowds that throng the spot
> Will still as usual complain
> That 'Here's the old familiar rot
> Again'.

III

Some years ago a public-spirited lady was proposing to make a
considerable benefaction to a California University—the State
University, if I remember. She was a woman of some definite
opinions; she disliked the Mormons; and, remembering how near

the State of Utah and Salt Lake City lie to California, and aware that young Mormons flocked over the borders, she suggested a clause that no Mormon should be eligible for scholarship or studentship founded by her gift. A shrewd professor said to her: 'You are wrong; Mormonism will lose more, if you admit young Mormons to the University scholarships than if you exclude them.' I hope I do not need to explain to readers that the dissenters of England neither practise polygamy nor even read the book of Mormon; but I incline to wonder whether the California professor's forecast might not have been illustrated from Cambridge. How many outstanding men in modern Cambridge would never have been here, but for the removal of the ban on dissenters? Of course, they are not dissenters now; their wives, their colleagues, their concentration on their special subjects of study, have changed all that. It might be difficult to decide whether the dissenting communities in the country have had any very clear gain from the 'opening' of the two older Universities; it is quite clear that the Universities have.

Along with this I would put the relaxation of the requirement of holy orders. Perhaps we have too few clergy to-day; there is a difficulty sometimes in finding them for College purposes; but it has strengthened College and University, over and over again, to be able to retain laymen on their staffs. With this too I would include the growing practice of recruiting a Cambridge staff from outside, from London or the United States, or wherever it be. There are limits here beyond which it is hardly desirable to go. The layman and the dissenter enter as freshmen, grow up together in the one atmosphere, and understand it. Too many men fetched from outside will do more than reinforce our intellectual or examination life; they will change the character of the place, which would be a pity. The great danger to the intellectual development of England to-day is standardization—one Board of Education, one B.B.C., one type of gramophone record, fewer newspapers of conflicting opinions, and the newspapers which are left to us controlled by big concerns or individuals, a Harmsworth, a Berry, or people progressively more like the American owners. It is an asset to England that Oxford is Oxford and Cambridge is Cambridge, and neither of them London or Birmingham, which supply the country with other types. We need a good many types, if education is not to become sterile. Central in education is challenge, which is perhaps the main deficiency in the great public schools of England and in the whole conception of education in America. A great type—the English public school boy; and it would be well for the Dominions and the United States if they could produce that type; but we want variety of types. As long as our imports do not too heavily re-model us, let us recruit our intellectual forces—but let it be our forces recruited, and not our special character and contribution obliterated. And I will recur to what I have already said, the great changes come unobserved. *Nemo repente fuit turpissimus*—a man, a nation, and a University are very rarely *suddenly* ruined; the ruin is apt to be the catastrophe, the culmination of changes long proceeding.

IV

Meanwhile Cambridge has during these years been recognizing in one way and another a wider world. Some years ago St John's College gave a dinner to Herbert Foxwell on his eightieth birthday. In a witty speech he thanked his entertainers, and spoke of one signal change he had seen. He looked up and down the long table and noted how many of his hosts were familiar with regions of the Empire, and indeed of the world, that in his undergraduate days no don dreamed of visiting; a 'high table' that knew—and knew intimately—New Zealand, Nigeria, Canada, yes! and the United States, was a new thing. In his youth people stayed on and on in Cambridge; if they went abroad, it was to France, Switzerland, Italy; I suppose a certain elect few knew India through the Indian Civil Service, Anglo-Indian forbears and like causes; but India was the one permitted exception to the limited range. Conversely, I suppose that to-day we have fewer Alpinists;

at least I do not hear of them; one hears oftener in fact of break-neck climbs by undergraduates over College roofs—not quite the wisest of possible diversions.

V

Lastly, after the first German war, a new Universities Commission made drastic endeavours to re-model Cambridge, top, bottom and middle. For centuries the centre of academic life had been the College (and a very good centre, too, with its diversities of types); now it was to be the 'faculty' (a group of people of one interest). We owed this to the scientific departments; they were each of them centred in huge buildings, more like government offices or factories than the old-time Colleges; their staffs were from every College; buildings were kept up and staffs paid largely by the taxation of College revenues which had been given for no such purposes. The 'lab' was really more to the new type of man than the College, and very often he came from outside and knew little of our traditions. The new statutes were inspired, if not drafted, by men of this make. All Cambridge was to be re-organized into 'faculties', even where there was and could be no 'lab', and where the essential teaching was man to man in College rooms. Theorists, reformers, and science men had their way; and men whose business was with history, language and literature were drastically herded into their several faculties. The ideal seemed to be the transformation of Cambridge into a copy of the huge American 'State University'—the triumph of practical efficiency over humanism, and the substitution of science for culture. The Colleges were not abolished; they were subordinated; in most cases it became impossible for a College to recruit its staff without the leave of a faculty board and pains seemed to have been taken to limit the freedom of a College, even (one might say) to secure a certain stigma for a College official as opposed to an employé of a faculty. Nor was this all.

Long ago A. E. H. Love, who left St John's to be professor at

Oxford, made the criticism that Cambridge after all was devoting herself chiefly to the production of professors. The newer ideal for a professor was devotion to 'research', which is very well in scientific studies, but less obviously useful in literature. Broadly speaking, in literature the less a professor 'researches' in the modern sense of the term the more likely he is to understand what he is doing. Manuscripts and antecedents are of little help to the real understanding of literature; and the substitution of palaeography for philosophy among theologians simply ruins the subject. However, we were in for scientific ideals, and research prevailed; and, to clinch things, professors were to be elected in a new way; eminent outsiders were to have a hand in the elections, who could be counted on to take an abstract view of the subject, uninformed and indifferent about our traditions, perhaps careless of the training of men, but ardent in the development of specialists. As a result we got a number of 'heads of departments', some of them no doubt specialists of high quality, some of them less eminent and more likely to stay in Cambridge for life. In America a University man gets promotion by moving from University to University between the Atlantic and the Pacific, ending, if he can, at Harvard, unless special inducements (the headship of a department for instance) hold him elsewhere.

Meantime, tenure of Fellowships—ignominiously called 'prize Fellowships'—was shortened and made dependent on the pursuit of 'research' of some kind; and the Colleges had larger numbers of short-term Fellows, sometimes married, fugitive phantoms who hovered about and disappeared without much chance of identification with the Colleges (sometimes not their own) which housed them. A College came to be a place where science men from the labs had free dinners, men very often who had been brought in from outside, and could not be expected to understand College feeling. The Colleges have very loyally tried to assimilate these men, electing them to Fellowships and giving them a share in College government. Yet there was at least one professor, thus brought in, to whom no College offered a Fellowship, and he lived and died with the consciousness, one supposes, that Cambridge, the inner Cambridge, did not want him. One can hardly imagine that he felt anything else; and one asks why he did not go; and the mind can only make a grim answer.

VI

Yet from time out of mind one of the main purposes of a University has been to train men 'to serve God in church and state' —citizens in fact; and it has been a happy feature of Cambridge College life that they were so trained (one might say) without knowing it. Moral lessons in poetry, so Charles Lamb told Wordsworth, should slide into the mind while it imagines no such thing. So with ideals generally; if the man is not to be priggish, he does better to absorb them unconsciously, from living alongside of the right people, let us say. (You may read something like this in Plato and in the Gospels.) A College, that is to say a High Table staffed by a denatured group of specialists from a score of alien laboratories, may not succeed any better at instilling citizenship than culture. But is the pure researcher likely to conceive of either task as his ideal? He comes from some other place altogether, is unfamiliar with our young men, and is often, we find, very imperfectly developed himself. Democratization of education is a great dream; but, when you wake, it is too often a sort of mass production. But education is really the play of soul on soul, the touch of spirit, something not communicable so readily as people think by lectures and laboratories; a closer contact, a more intimate relation, is needed. Happily the Colleges, in one way and another, have managed to find in some measure the men they need; and happily a Ph.D., if caught young, can be tamed. 'We have to remember', said the Oxford man of the famous story, 'that even Cambridge men are God's creatures'; and we have to remember it, too, about our adopted colleagues. The undergraduate, when proper contacts are established, is a very humanizing person, as I hope to suggest in the chapter that follows.

We have many more undergraduates than we used to have; and they also show the ravages of time. Probably there will be fewer men, and perhaps many fewer cars, after this war. Fifty years ago men who had money and wished for amusement (or to challenge the Proctors) would drive tandems, against which the University fulminated in one edict and another; to-day how many people have ever seen horses driven tandem? The Union has decayed, one judges—abandoned very largely to Indians and communists; it has a bar where the up-to-date young man can take the Newnhamite for a drink and 'elevenses'. Debating does not flourish as it once did; Socialist and Labour clubs advertise themselves freely, but that is not the same thing.

But after two experiences of Proctorship—and unusual ones, I may say, covering the year before the first war, the first year of that war, and again between the armistice and the peace, and the strange year following the peace—neither period thus being of the average length but both periods very unlike normal times— I am left with a great admiration of the Cambridge undergraduate. I offer no very clear view as to whether there is any great improvement or the reverse in conduct, moral judgment, religion or intellectual freedom among them since my time. Cars, crosswords, cinema and wireless do not inevitably promote the thoughtful life; but it is quite clear that they have not destroyed it altogether. I have seen a good deal of American College life, East, West, and Central; and in spite of all the charm and courtesy of American hospitality as you so often meet it, I feel the balance of advantage is with our own youth; their minds are less childish, their humour less commonplace, their manners better. The English home is a more real thing; the English public school, with all its limitations, is better than the very different 'public school' of America; the standards of education seem to me to be solider; and the Cambridge College, in spite of imports and Ph.D.'s, research and practical people, is still a nursery of culture and character.

And now let us leave the High Table—and the laboratory—and come back to the undergraduate, who, when all is said, is the real centre of everything in any University—the *raison d'être*, if you like a French phrase, the problem, the difficulty, the joy of the place; and my last chapter shall be about him and his nonsensical ways—ways which experience endorses—*dulce est...*—but you will remember what Horace wrote to Virgil.

Chapter VI

UNDERGRADUATE

To be tiresome, it has been said, it is only necessary to discuss education. Is there a subject on which men are more apt to be tedious? We generalize swiftly when education is mentioned, each of us deliberately or unconsciously basing himself upon his own experience; and the more magnificent our systems and theories grow, the less relation they seem to bear to life. The fact is, very few of us are really educated at all, and those who are best educated seem, like the best men elsewhere, to wish least to dogmatize about it. The men who go furthest are often the worst at mapping the route. There are critics who tell us that the route offered by one of the older English Universities does not take us very far and, moreover, leads us in the wrong direction. I will not dispute with them. All I will say is that it is a very pleasant route, and that one falls in with fellow-travellers upon it, who are human in a very large and delightful way—some indeed who are less human—but so many who grow progressively great of heart and wide of sympathy, that one feels at least that with all its defects—its failure to achieve the last thought in macadamizing, for instance—it must be a road that trends to the right goal, however many others there are.

The distinguishing feature of the older English Universities—for it has to be remembered there are two—is their preservation of the ancient system of College life. There are alternatives to this. Men group themselves elsewhere in other ways—by the year in which they enter the University or by that in which they expect to graduate (the class of 1900 which I found as newly arrived as myself in the Canadian University was known as Noughty-Nought)—by the subjects of their choice, such as theology,

8-2

medicine, arts or horse-doctoring—by age or wealth or religion or their views on politics, which form the bases of many combinations, e.g. the 'fraternities' of American Colleges. But one may be pardoned for thinking that the English College system has advantages over them all. Here are grouped, and here are working together, men of every origin, of different ages and 'subjects', of the widest varieties in wealth and religion, educating one another without knowing that they are doing it, and that perhaps is one of the great secrets of real education. The nucleus of College life is the staircase, and it branches out into the boat club, dinner in hall, College chapel, the lecture-room, and all sorts of things. Of this life I propose to give such a picture as I may be able to draw of memories of the late 'eighties and the early 'nineties, helped out by illustrations from what historians impressively call contemporary sources.

I

The staircase may be old and inconvenient, an ancient and awkward monument of days when no one thought a grand piano a necessity—a twisting and unsafe ascent to rooms as ill-conceived, dark, low-ceiled and cramped. Or it may be a modern affair with air and light, with big windows and stone steps, leading to rooms planned for comfort and even for convenience. Over every staircase and its six or eight sets of rooms was appointed a bedmaker, as to whom, legend says, the ancient statutes prescribed that she should be old and ugly. Indeed, one might guess that Touchstone had some such place in mind for Audrey, when he said: 'Praised be the gods for thy foulness! sluttishness may come hereafter.' 'The courts', wrote a man a little after my period, 'are full of squalid hags, who squeak and gibber, as they carry home their purloined bread.' The queer old horse tram that went along King's Parade and eventually reached East Road had a permanent smell about it of old bread; it was the bedmaker's homeward route; to-day she appears to have taken to the bicycle, which implies that she is not so old as she once was. The bedmaker had her perquisites. A fourpenny loaf came every morning, and not a quarter of it was eaten by the freshman. In return for this and other things of the kind, for a stated wage paid by the College and recovered from the student, and a variable tip, which custom always strove to fix, she looked after the rooms—'keeping room', bedroom and gyp-room—and generally maintained a reasonable dead level of neglect. Her husband might be the 'gyp'—a word of disputed origin, 'Egyptian or vulturous'—her partner in mess and petty larceny of victuals, and her tyrant. Here I may begin to quote *The Granta* of those days from which I shall have to draw a good deal:

Should your bedmaker carelessly soil
    The books you have left on your table
With candle-grease, blacking or oil,
    You should bear it as well as you're able—
Yet the mildest of Junior Deans
Will at times give his bedmaker beans.

If your carpet is mostly unswept,
    (And your gyp isn't likely to sweep it),
If your room is disgracefully kept
    (And that's how your bedder will keep it),
They are but adding fuel to fire
Who tell you to bottle your ire.

Elsewhere we read a man's scheme of a special purgatory for his acquaintance:

And, first of all, it were fit to begin
With my gyp, that hardened man of sin,—
My gyp's long score to the full were paid
Might he lie for aye on a bed he had made.

A satirist, even if he writes from knowledge, is generally conceded by literary critics a right to limit himself in the use of truth.

It is also true that these elderly women were often decent kindly creatures. If they were not always miracles of cleanliness, they were often careful of the health and comfort of their 'gentlemen', believed in well-aired beds and warm rooms, and insisted on having such notice, when men were coming up, as would allow these natural comforts to be achieved. Too often they were the victims of husbands who married them to be supported by their earnings, and the woman who was dismal enough as a wife would brighten up wonderfully as a widow.

The undergraduate owned everything in his rooms. He took over at a valuation what his predecessor left—or refused it, in which case the valuer had to take it—and then he added what he thought fit, chairs, bookcases, pictures, crockery, table-silver, brooms and pans for the gyp-room, pipe-racks, curtains, ornaments and so forth. The Cambridge shops every October laid themselves out to suit him. In particular, cheap pictures filled their windows to catch his eye with their innocent and sentimental art.

Along with the problems of furnishing came those of dress, where many pitfalls awaited the unwary. He might find cap and gown provided in his room—an enterprising tailor had made friends with the 'bedder'. How long ought the tassel to be on his square cap? Just so long as not to hang over at any point. Should he slit the sleeves of his gown? Some Colleges did; some did not. Here is advice from *The Granta*: 'You may smoke in academical dress, assault policemen, insult your Dean, dye the town vermilion, even come in after twelve, and all will be forgiven you. But there are some things you may not do. If you once go wrong, it will be no excuse to plead ignorance.... You may be ill-treated, for instance, if you wear gloves with your academical dress, but you will probably not be regarded as a leper for the rest of your days. ...When a senior man, who was a freshman himself only last year, calls on you, you must not resent his air of patronage. Do not content yourself with leaving a card on his bedmaker by way of return for his favours. You must knock at the great man's

door, until you find him in.... Above all, if you should happen to
have grown a beard between the time of your leaving school and
coming up here, cut it off and cast it from you. You will be better
liked without it.'

For you, says one of *The Granta's* many poets:

> For you the tradesman spreads his show,
>   The tout prepares his artful games;
> The lynx-eyed porter sees you go
>   Across the grass, and notes your names.
>
> All life you fully understand,
>   Yet freshmen walk our streets again
> With gloved umbrella-bearing hand
>   Held high to guard their gowns from rain;
>
> And some—the jest hath freshness still
>   Though cynics sneer and gyps deride—
> Perchance will mount the ancient hill
>   To see their freshmen's term divide.

In these passages we have a well-marked line drawn between
actions banned by Parliament, the Town Council and the University, and on the other hand those actions which, as Thucydides
—or Pericles in his pages—said, are forbidden by 'unwritten laws,
the breaking of which brings admitted shame'.

II

The undergraduate in Cambridge has much less freedom in
some directions than in the Scottish or the American University.
The courts, as we more accurately call what Oxford in defiance
of Euclid misnames quadrangles, are generally adorned with grass
plots, carefully nurtured. Only dons are allowed to walk on the
grass, and they do it with discretion. Here is a point at which that
conflict with ancient rule may begin that so often heralds progress.
The College porter watches over the grass plot and reports
trespasses to the Dean, unless—unless he doesn't for some un-

specified reason. In old days he had other things to report, as an old Cambridge alphabet shows:

> G is my gown: chuck it off! it's eleven!
> H 'Half-a-crown, Sir! it's ten fifty-seven!'

Other regions remain where he is still eyes and ears to the Dean—in the chapel where he marks attendance, still compulsory in my youth, a century after Wordsworth's criticism of it in *The Prelude*—at the gate, where he notes the moment of every man's return after 10 p.m.—and on nights when bonfires are planned. 'Called emphatically men' (Calverley's phrase), the men do things which in later life seem a little youthful. *Homo Sapiens, desipiens in loco*, was Tottenham's definition of our kind in those days. So the College porter had his place—and his opportunities, as was sometimes suggested.

> 'You are old,' said the youth, 'as I mentioned before,
> And I find, when two chapels I've done,
> That, though you incessantly stand at the door,
> You have managed to mark them as one.'

> 'It is so, but observe,' Mr Muddles replied,
> 'That I balance my score with much trouble,
> My enemies' chapels by two I divide,
> That my friends' I may manage to double.'

Here again libel is not all the truth. For loyalty to the College and its sons, few would be harder to beat than some of the porters. They never forget us, and they recognize us, when, after years of absence, we return bald as a condor, bearded as a pard. One famous head porter, Stoakley of Pembroke, was a great gardener, who kept his College court beautiful beyond all others—a grave, stern, good old man, whom I like to recall as a friend of mine. Others are cheery souls, whose role in life is helpfulness, varied by strict attention to the Dean's wishes. And now it is time that we went and 'saw the Dean'.

'A fogey' revisits Cambridge and tells his reminiscences in an early *Granta*. 'Dick is a Lancashire rector now, with a barren glebe and a fruitful wife'; but in undergraduate days, fresh together

> We both wore gloves with our cap and gown,
> And umbrellas too in showery weather,
> And on Guy Fawkes day we challenged the town
> And gave and received black eyes together.

> We both cut chapels and stayed out late—
> I wonder if Dick can still play loo;
> Could he climb, I wonder, the New Court gate,
> As—I blush to confess it—we used to do?

> We both bought wine and cigars (on tick)
> And both with money were far too free,
> And the Dean was often 'at home' to Dick,
> He was just as often 'at home' to me.

And, as another humourist suggested, the Dean would arrange for his visitors to be 'At Home' too, by the week together. For, when disorder reached a certain pitch, the Dean would 'gate' a man at such an hour (let us say 8 p.m.) for such a period, which meant that he must be within the College by 8 p.m. every night, or in his lodgings, if he lodged in the town.[1] A man in College had, even if gated, certain opportunities of life and human intercourse in his friends' rooms, if he did not know any private ways into College. There were ways—by the bridge and the window next it, if you knew the man for instance—or over the back gate, as we have seen. The man gated in lodgings was in worse case; he was dependent on good Samaritans who remembered him and called; for the landlord depended for his living on the strict use of his key.

The functions of a Dean, it will be seen, did not offer him many chances of cheap popularity, and not all Deans were equally

---

1 Cambridge men will not need this explanation, but they will perhaps forgive my offering it to friends overseas, who have not our advantages. See *The Granta* (quoted in the next paragraph) on the sad state of Scottish Universities.

successful in using the chances they had. Then there might come big trouble, and the comfortable way out was a College living, or some other promotion.

> Upon a time there was a Dean;
>   No Dean was so undeanly.
> His methods could not worse have been;
>   He managed things so meanly—
> Not outward things; his dress was neat,
>   No tattered coat, nor frayed hose,
> Adorned his frame whom now we name
>   Lord Bishop of Barbados.
>
> He had a knack of falling out
>   With men of every pattern;
> His horoscope beyond a doubt
>   Betrayed the reign of Saturn;
> Upon the peacefullest of scenes
>   He'd burst like ten tornadoes;
> But our undeanliest of deans
>   Is Bishop of Barbados.

Historically—for here I know the names—he was not Bishop of anything. 'Don,' said an earlier writer in *Light Green*, 'a short way of spelling all that is unpleasant in man; Dean, a nastier way.' 'The men who keep our consciences', wrote someone in *The Granta*, 'may be classics and wranglers of high degree and nevertheless they may understand nothing of human nature'; and he speaks sensibly of compulsory chapel: 'The moral effects on the Dean's victims are appalling. Compulsion ends in repulsion. Many a man on going down celebrates his independence by leaving the Church of his fathers.' And then he concludes happily: 'Against Deans in their other capacities I throw no stone. Discipline is necessary; without it we should sink to the level of the Scottish universities, which can never know the pleasure of breaking rules because they have none to break. So long as they are content to preserve good order and green turf and regular hours, Deans are certainly to be encouraged. But in connection with compulsory chapels they are misguided fanatics, and enemies of true religion.'

'I'm your enemy,' a witty Dean used to say to undergraduates; 'it's your Tutor who's your friend.' For in Cambridge Tutor does not mean—at least with a capital T—what it does at Oxford, a person who merely looks over exercises. Our Latinity is purer. The entrance examination or 'Littlego' [1] in Cambridge is officially called the Previous, and the Tutor is guardian as the Latin would suggest. He is *in loco parentis*,[2] it is always said; he recommends courses of reading and prescribes lectures, he takes charge of you in case of illness or emergency, he bails you out of the police station, he stands up for you when the Dean becomes unreasonable. On the other hand, if the Dean is right, and if your conduct leaves too far behind the standards desired by the College, he will send you down. But as long as you are 'up', you and your Tutor work together. The Tutor and the undergraduate form the strongest combination in the University when easy access is sought to the B.A. degree; between them they find out the 'soft options', and the Tutor is always on the outlook on University boards and councils to safeguard his charge against excessive demands upon industry or intelligence. We did not know that when we were young. No wonder Tutors have testimonials when they retire; as the poet said,

> Gorgeous present he got;
> Silver, I reckon, not pewter;
> Sugar-tongs and a teapot-
> Showed our respect for our tutor.

One feature of College discipline, which may surprise people outside, is the requirement that every undergraduate dines at least five nights in the week in the College hall. It makes for the common life; it secures that the poorest man has nutriment at

1 It is sad to be told that this time-honoured name is no longer familiar, except to antiquaries.
2 I since learn that this phrase to-day is taken as the Latin equivalent of 'modern daughter'. 'Modern father' is surely *ex-post-facto*.

least once a day, for his other meals he looks after himself in his own rooms; and it helps to secure that the student really is in Cambridge. Cambridge degrees depend on residence; a man must reside so many days in each term if he is to 'keep the term', and he needs nine terms for his degree. Dining in hall is considered a help toward this. It is a matter of faith with undergraduates—or was—that the dinner is a bad one. They would grumble at the meat, at the 'caterpillary attraction' of the vegetables, at the gooseberries used for the tart. The last formed the gravamen of a petition to a College steward, entitled '*De Disgustibus*', which was drawn up about 1890 but perhaps not presented formally. It began:

> Sir, we're not ambitious
> For a choice of dishes;
> Upon loaves and fishes,
>   Were they fresh and clean,
> You might safely trust to
> Us to feed with gusto,
> Until fit to bust a
>   'Try-your-weight' machine.

The poet surveys the dinner item by item, wishes 'the dickens had those ancient chickens' and so forth and then concentrates on the gooseberries:

> Oh! if we could see 'em
> In the Fitz Museum,
> What a great Te Deum
>   We would shout aloud!
> So send those berries
> To the Antiquaries,
> Or manure the prairies
>   With your fragrant store;
> And your petitioners
> Will pray like missioners,
> Nor need physician-ers
>   For ever more.

III

Perhaps by now it is time to refer in passing to the lectures and the lecture-rooms, where some would find the very centre of Cambridge life. It must be owned they were sometimes dull enough, and they need not take up space here. Lectures everywhere are much the same, and Cambridge is in this very like other places. One point may be noted however. There were two ways to a degree—one by Honours and a Tripos, the other the Poll (abridged from οἱ πολλοί). The Honours man, when he was done with his Previous, was troubled no more by the University with examinations till he took the Tripos for which he specialized. The Poll man had his way punctuated with two parts of a General Examination before he reached his Special, also in two parts. (Hence Tottenham's suggestion that 'his General is caviare to him'.) A Tripos candidate is not asked to construe at a lecture; it is not a 'recitation'; he sits, listens and takes notes, or occupies his time as best he may; and he may not come out. It is not done. It has been done by slipping between desk and bench on to the floor, while the lecturer read from his manuscript, and then after an interval quietly crawling out. But enough of this part of our subject; as someone wrote, with a hint of indebtedness to Wordsworth:

Lectures are but a sleep and a forgetting.

Let us forget them and try a little more of the variety of Cambridge life.

Our backs and bridges, bills and bells,
Our boats and bumps and bloods and blues,
Our bedders, bull-dogs and Bedells,
Our chapels, colleges, canoes,
Our dons and deans and duns and dues,
Our friends from Hayti and Siam,
Tinge with kaleidoscopic hues
This ancient city by the Cam.

Cambridge by day is a commonplace country town of yellow brick—apart from the Colleges—of duns and bills and shop windows. By night the streets have a new point of interest, as we are reminded again and again in *The Granta*'s pages.

> O Proctor dear, where are you roaming?
> O would that I could hear you coming,
>   As I sing both high and low.
> Come not near me, I've been dining;
> Dinners end in Proctors fining,
>   Every undergrad doth know.

'On the whole,' says a leader-writer in the same columns, 'we recommend a serious demeanour *vis-à-vis* of a Proctor. Always remember that, if he has fairly cornered you, he has quite two to one the better of you. Indeed, the University Statutes lay it down that in cases of breaches of discipline, if there be *quid gravius*, the Proctor may increase the fine; and a thoughtless word has been known under such circumstances to cost an additional six and eightpence. Remember too, that the Proctor is not always a bad fellow....Only take to your heels when you are quite certain not to be caught.'

> And one great evening, I call to mind,
>   When Proctor and bull-dogs gave us chase;
> Dick was noisy, we both had dined;
>   And they ran us down in the Market Place.
>
> But oh! what a race we had of it first,
>   Petty Cury, Parade, and forrard again,
> Through Senate House Passage, and then with a burst
>   Into Trinity Street through Trinity Lane.
>
> And then with our haven well in sight,
>   When we thought we had done with our vain alarms,
> Before we had time to turn left or right,
>   We found ourselves in the Proctor's arms.

The Proctor's duties in those days were not quite the same as now. He had a civil jurisdiction over the streets, and certain characters he could arrest and commit to the Spinning House. But about 1890 this part of his work was transferred to the town police—not unhappily. The Proctors were also concerned to check tandem-driving, which is long out of fashion in Cambridge. Instead, the Proctors have had of late years heavy work in the survey of cinema shows and in the registration and control of motor-cars and motor-cycles kept by students. Six hundred were registered in one winter before the first German war. The main work of the Proctor was moral discipline, and the streets and the cars came naturally under his care. From about 8 p.m. to midnight there was always one Proctor, sometimes more, on patrol. Two men, traditionally known as Bull-dogs and supposed to be fleet of foot, men with a wide and peculiar knowledge of who's who and who isn't, go with him, wearing tall hats, which are as conspicuous as the white bands and cap and gown of the Proctor. All students are required to wear cap and gown after dark, and to have them in good order; and the enforcement of this rule and of another of ancient years against smoking in academical dress is the point at which the Proctor and the undergraduate most frequently come in contact. The smoking rule is an old and rather vexatious one, and some Proctors, while they enforce it, as they must, lean to extenuating circumstances.

> He'll come if you don't wear your gown, and stay out rather late,
> He'll put you in his little book and fine you six and eight.
> He'll catch you when you're smoking after dark, that's if he sees,
> He'll mildly doff his cap and say, 'Your name and College, please!'
> And in the morn the Bull-dog comes, you pay him if you can.

The 5th of November was in old days a night consecrated to disorder, to bonfires and fireworks and to fights between town and gown. By 1890 the vigour of the warfare was declining, but freshmen went out together and fought any townees who were available. All the six Proctors would be occupied the whole evening. One point may be noted as characteristic. Whatever spirit was put into the game of outwitting the Proctor, if the townees attempted to touch him, the situation was changed, his victims rallied to him and fought the town to save him from indignity. This is a Cambridge tradition; our quarrels are within the family. Thus, in a certain College, opinion was dissatisfied with the dinner in hall, and a two-nights' boycott took place. A London half-penny paper sent a reporter to write it up. 'If you want to know about our hall,' said the boycotters politely, 'you should go and see the Steward'—they would not give him away. In the twentieth century Guy Fawkes day declined into still lower depths of inanity and silliness—the burning of a haystack, and aimless processions of freshmen escorted by street boys, and nothing done beyond the discharge of fireworks.

A Cambridge humourist once spoke of perennial jokes that please every generation in turn—mother-in-law or policeman, for example. In Cambridge it has been Proctor. One of the happiest suggestions on the subject was the proposed addition to the Oxford and Cambridge sports of a Proctors' Coursing Match. Two undergraduates smoking in cap and gown were to be liberated from traps, and the Proctor who first secured his man and took his name and College was to be held to have won the event for his University.

IV

At the period of which I speak, athletics were in full swing. Every College had its boat club—the Lady Margaret Boat Club of St John's being the oldest—and a movement was in progress for blending all the athletic clubs in each College into an Amalgamation Club. Finance lay behind this move. The Boat Club was a costly affair, the others were inexpensive by comparison, and the amalgamation helped to maintain the boats. On the boats again and again depended the repute of the College, and it was not, as things go, such a bad test. For a College boat to maintain for years together a good place on the river, the College must have a perpetual succession of good, sound, healthy-natured men, loyal and enthusiastic for their College. The Cam is a narrow stream, and the principal of bumping races was borrowed or invented to meet the case. The boats rowed one behind another; the winning boat bumped that ahead of it, and next day they changed places. The races lasted four days, and when a boat went up four places, a place a day, the men received their oars, painted with the College arms and the names of the crew, as trophies—these to keep. Each afternoon following one on which a bump was made the victorious crew wore flowers in their hats.

The boat took precedence of football and cricket in College interest, and these of hockey, lacrosse and golf. Golf was hardly played at that time. To represent the College in some sport was the common ambition—hence the sting of these lines:

> I am not athletic at all,
>   Nor destined by Nature for sport;
> My biceps is certainly small
>   And my sight is excessively short.
>
> I never was partial to balls
>   Or the games which are played by their aid;
> For the danger, which others enthrals,
>   Unluckily makes me afraid.
>
> There are some love to smite them with bats,
>   And to hurl them at parallel sticks;
> Some serve them with entrails of cats,
>   Some pursue them with violent kicks.

Nor does the gentleman row, but he begs not to be condemned unheard, or to be regarded as a 'smug'—

> For one touch can make us all kin;
>   One weakness I too must confess—
> I very soon hope to begin
>   To play for my College at chess.

References to the river pervade the talk and the journals of the time. Here is the 'Lament of an Oarsman'—with that suggestion

of Robert Browning's metre and manner that abounds in the
verse of that day:

> Oh! who's for the river? The sleet drives cold,
>   And the wind bites shrewdly, the clouds are black,
> (The proper expression for this, I'm told,
>   Is 'The sky is o'ercast with the tempest's wrack'.)
>
> And the rain falls swift, and the stream is slow,
>   And the scent of the river is wafted strong,
> And life is short—is it right to row
>   In weather like this on a slide that's long?
>
> Barnwell Pool is dreary and dank,
>   The birthplace of smells and the grave of hope;
> Would his death be swift if a man once drank
>   This oozy mixture of slime and soap?
>
> Down we drift in a labouring eight,
>   And we stir the Cam to its utmost dregs;
> And the coach from his horse shouts 'Bow, you're late,
>   Sit up, don't bucket, and use your legs'.
>
> And the casual 'funny' runs down the pair,
>   And both are upset by a Freshman's four—
> Four and a cox; with their eyes a-stare—
>   'Hi! look ahead Sir! Mind your oar!'

Then follows the rowing of a 'course', and the poet concludes
with a growl:

> So these are our joys, and this our toil;
>   And this is truth that I now record;
> Rowing is—what with blister and boil,
>   And the rain and the sewers—its own reward.
>
> Yet every day it is just the same
>   Though my nose be red and my fingers blue,
> I visit the river and sink my name
>   And become one-eighth of an eight-oared crew.

The last line puts the great feature of the discipline. No man
in the boat ever won the race by himself—not even the lady.

novelist's oarsman who rowed distinctly quicker than the rest of
the crew—but almost any man could lose it for the boat. To row
for one's College was service where the individual and his glory
were sunk, where College spirit endured what the poet has just
told us for the sake of the College as much as for any pleasure in
the thing. There were no heroics, and no escape once in the boat.
It was discipline, and a valuable one—it called for skill and
patience, it trained in co-operation and it denied (except in rare
cases) any individual halo. And for those who threw themselves
into it, there was more.

They cannot know who lounge and loaf the fierce exultant glow
That warms the heart and stirs the pulse when eight men really row,
When the banks go mad with roaring, and the roar becomes a yell,
And the bow-men feel her dancing as she lifts upon the swell;
And the crowd in chaos blending rend the welkin with advice;
'Swing out, you've gained, you're gaining, you must get them in a trice';
Till with one last stroke we do it, and the coxswain's face grows bright
And it's 'Easy all, my bonny boys, you've made your bump to-night!'
I met a solid rowing friend, and asked about the race,
'How fared it with your wind?' I said, 'when stroke increased the pace?
You swung it forward mightily, you heaved it greatly back;
Your muscles rose in knotted lumps, I almost heard them crack.
And while we roared and rattled too, your eyes were fixed like glue,
What thoughts were flying through your mind, how fared it, Five, with
    you?'
But Five made answer solemnly, 'I heard them fire a gun,
No other mortal thing I knew until the race was done.'

Another line of interest and ambition marked the Union. Here
great questions were solemnly debated week by week—humorously, too—and men cultivated style and in some cases learnt to
speak in such a way that their rising was not followed by the
immediate exit of the assembly. Week by week the debates were
reported, and the speakers criticized, in the University papers.
'Mr Blank gave some successful imitations of a crowing cock and
a screaming child.' It was supposed—or hoped—that success at
the bar or in Parliament might await our leading speakers, but it

did not. My generation of Cambridge has not been markedly more successful in politics than in poetry; we have had no Lord Chancellor any more than we had a Rupert Brooke. Still, the Union too was education. Here are a few lines of advice given by someone reporting at the Union, and they would be hard to better. 'The successful speaker in the Union is he who speaks unpretentiously, shortly, naturally and earnestly; who does not mistake platitude for thought, or cheap vulgarity for wit; who does not affect a force he does not feel; who does not think his few words a necessity for every debate; and, finally, who does not speak for more than seven minutes after ten o'clock.'

Of political clubs, of the A.D.C. and the Footlights, of the Greek play, a good deal might be said, but will not be; but a corner may be spared for the Grantchester 'grind'. The London road going south from Cambridge is not unpleasant with the great bank of trees on the right hand, and it leads to the village of Trumpington, where Chaucer placed his mill. Modern Cambridge men believe he meant Grantchester, famous long before in the Venerable Bede—another village half a mile or more away to the westward, where the road winds through fields, and by the stream flowing down from Byron's pool, and past the mill and its open water, the scene, we all believed, of Tennyson's poem *The Miller's Daughter* and worthy of it. Then we turned off to the right and crossed a series of open meadows, with the Cam, here known as the Granta, slowly finding its way down to Cambridge. It is a beautiful walk for this country, but I speak of it here for it was a good part, in old days before low [1] bicycles and motor-cycles, of undergraduate life. Here we walked out in twos, talking, arguing, disputing and enjoying ourselves—and learning a great deal as we went, of tolerance and genial sense and strange opinions. Such intercourse will never die till Cambridge is reformed out of all life—no, not even in these days of wheels; but

---

1 I see this is a term of ambiguous suggestion. It was meant in antithesis to 'high' bicycles, which people, only five or six years my senior, had still been riding.

I doubt if it would ever be so good indoors and at late hours as in the afternoons on the Grantchester meadows.

The staircase, as I said before, was the nucleus of College life—six or eight rooms, and in them lived how many types? You lived at the top and read Classics; the man opposite was a mathematician from Aberdeen; under you was a Chinese medical student from Singapore or a Jap or an Indian; under him a Poll man meaning to be ordained and reform the universe; below were the College drunkard, a Science man perhaps, a 'Moral Stinks' man, and the First Boat Captain; and among you you represented four or five academic years and held eight varieties of religious belief, and as many of temperament, almost as many shades of politics, and of taste or no-taste in literature. You entertained one another at tea, borrowed milk and money, and furniture for entertainments, introduced your sisters (and sometimes —if grammar will stand it—you married them in the long run). We had to live together. We had our own sets of rooms and had as many meals alone as we chose, or shared them as we pleased. But we were one body, a microcosm—we had to pull together to keep the boat club going, and the College magazine, and the debating society and a lot more things—in short, the College. The dons, of course, did something in their detached and uncomfortable way; but we were the College. (When one reached the High Table, this conviction seemed to require modification.)

'Cambridge', said a writer in *The Granta*, 'is a great leveller. The lad who at school overtopped his fellows, has to step down from his pinnacle and become even as other men. The neglected schoolboy, who withered at school amidst the unsympathetic society of those who dubbed him mad, merely because he wore side-spring boots or valued the affection of a tame guinea-pig more than the rude society of human wild animals, finds sympathy and appreciation. He can wear his hair long without being cuffed, and read English poetry without being sneered at or running the danger of an imposition. Even Peers leave their coronets behind them in their ancestral halls, and consent to wear the cap which

Proctors worship and rowdy men batter. Sometimes they are pilled for clubs—which is revolutionary; occasionally they fall off horses—which is absurd. But they no longer strut in the gold and purple wherewith the Cambridge of the past delighted to honour them. We have even seen a Peer whose cuffs were frayed, and who, in spite of the four columns in which Burke had chronicled his ancestry, was turned out of a Lent Boat for sugaring like any commoner. The Dean and the Examiner make no distinction between the proud and the lowly, the wealthy and the poor.'

The man made his place for himself. Of course, there were in a human society men who somehow or other were early 'boomed' and caught the eye of the student world. There were others who made their way more slowly to the front, but who got there by sheer manhood and worth, and no one asked whether they were scholars or sizars, or who their parents were. And with all the folly and nonsense we talked, with all the traditions and prejudices we called principles, men really did gravitate to deeper views of life, thought things out slowly and half-unconsciously, and re-shaped the courses they had planned. It came, I suppose, as much as anything, from the men we met—more than from the lectures we attended. So it always will be in Universities, but our College seemed to increase our chance of having our dogmatism broken up and our being put at a more universal point of view—if I may borrow language which we never dreamed of using.

Cambridge is apt to be cool where Oxford is hot. Oxford's most characteristic contribution to the nineteenth century was Newman; Cambridge gave Darwin, and said less about it. We leant rather to rationalism than romanticism, and took things coolly and quietly. What were the facts? Was there any sense in the thing? One small symptom was the very small place taken by the essay in our education, compared with the large place given to it at Oxford. It had too little attention, if truth must be told; and our bias to fact might degenerate sadly into 'common sense' without imagination. But we checked any tendency to gush that we saw in one another; and we corrected our views cautiously when we found them wrong. Here the lectures of the dons and the talk of our friends worked together; the same tone, allowing for age and responsibility, touched both. The extreme Low Churchmen were many and were little touched by the spirit of the place; the rest of us suffered something in enthusiasm and consecration, if we gained too by the constant reference to the facts of the case. Of poetry, apart from the type that I have been quoting, we wrote little—or did not mention it if we did. I am not sure that the twentieth-century Cambridge poets, with their anthologies of themselves and their friends, and their enthusiasm for their art, are really a very great improvement on my contemporaries. I doubt, too, if they will last; but middle-aged people are apt to have doubts of that sort, and by now I cannot be called middle-aged. The doubts are often justified, but perhaps it is kinder not to air them.

<h2 style="text-align:center">V</h2>

But to return to history, three years at Cambridge brought a man to his Tripos—the theme of many versifiers in *The Granta*, in strains that recall the poets from Keats to Browning. They begin with being called early on the examination day, and admonish gyp or bedder—

> You needn't pull the clothes off; I shall hear you as you tread
> With those great heavy feet of yours tramping round about my bed—

Or, like Keats with Cortés at Darien—for Cortés was rarely at Darien without Keats—

> I watched the men,
> Who, like myself o'erwhelmed with wild surprise,
> Sat silent chewing gloomily their pen—

Or, with Horace, deprecate cramming—

> Seek not, dear boy, to overstrain
> The intellect for this exam,
> Nor gauge amiss the gastric pain
> That comes of undigested cram;
> Nor ask the heathenish Chaldee
> For tips in pure Theology—

Or reflect how much better Cambridge is out-of-doors in the
month of May than in the Senate House, which is quite true if
irrelevant, for it is the best month of the year.

> The air is warm, and the sun glows bright,
>   And sweet and soft is the whispering breeze,
> A book and a boat in the Backs invite—
>   This is the season to take one's ease,
>   Lulled to sleep by the murmur of bees.—
> Why should I value a printed list?
>   Who cares twopence about degrees?
> Why is the Tripos allowed to exist?—

Or, somewhat like Wordsworth's soul, they face the ordeal

> In too entire forgetfulness
> And utter mental nakedness—

Or tell the whole story with the prolixity of *The Ring and the
Book*:

> What, Sir? You come thence? Then you're just my man!
> Bless us and save us! Why! myself I sat
> A week—six blessed live-by-labour days—
> There in the Senate House. Boh! what a time!
> What days, i' fegs, of brainpan-walloping!
> 'Grr!' whirrs alarm; 'Past eight!' bawls bedmaker.
> Out o' the bed you bundle, splash in tub,
> Heap clothes on, cram down breakfast, bolt away,
> And at the toll o' the bell, why, there you sit,
> As though you'd grown upon the very spot
> And never meant to budge an inch in life.
> Eye runs o'er paper, hand goes up to chin,
> Head nods approval or shakes woefulness.
> Then pen to page, and scribble all you know—
> Scratch head for breathing space—till twelve o'clock.
> 'Boom!' goes St Mary's, and you trundle out,
> Glad to be rid o' a twelfth o' the whole week's work—
> Run home to lunch—(or luncheon, do you say?
> Nay! as *you* please—pay money and take choice!)
> Stuff maw and mind together,—bread and book—
> And back again for all the afternoon.

When the Triposes are over—or are beginning to be less thick on the ground—the May Week follows, but in June. (College Examinations were called 'Mays', being held in March or June in our time, but not in May.)

> They say that Cambridge in the May
> Is at its very, very best,
> With all the crews in bright array,
> And all the damsels gaily drest;
>
> When every man has people up,
> And sisters, cousins, friends unite
> To fill the Undergraduate's cup
> With every possible delight;
>
> When matutinal tennis reigns
> And boats take up the afternoon;
> And every country maid complains
> The evenings are so short in June
>
> With supper hurried and scarce done
> Before a concert claims its due,
> And then a ball, till one by one
> The larks are high in heaven's blue.

It was all only too true. Tennis was allowed in the mornings, and girls played on our courts; and the May races took place in the afternoons. Of the boats we have spoken; the spectators packed in rowing-boats and dogcarts, were massed along the bank and in the paddock, at Ditton; and here we find them with some memories of Milton in his Cambridge days.

> Cam from his muddy bed
> Lifts an amazéd head
> To see his stream alive with ladies fair;
> While parasols, bedight
> With many a riband bright,
> Fling an unearthly radiance through the air,
> As shouts of exultation
> Escort each crew to its appointed station.

But hark! the last gun sounds,
And forward each boat bounds,
Swept by the eightfold stroke of racing oars,[1]
To win eternal fame
Or sully its fair name,
While either bank sends thunderous applause,
And inharmonious symphony
Of horns and rattles makes heart-piercing melody.

Nor less when Sol retires
Before the starry fires,
Doth joy still hold its universal sway.
In every College hall
At concert or at ball
The mirth of night outdoes the gladness of the day;
And Hymen, too, I ween
Doth oft attend the dance, a deity serene.

'Proposals of marriage' says one chronicler of such a ball, 'were thick as blackberries.' Perhaps they were not all accepted. I hope not.

Apart from halls and balls, there was endless entertainment in college rooms—the menus the unflinching choice of the hosts, and the result profits to the College kitchens.

White-robed, in the cool of the evening,
You gleam on the redolent gloom;
From the court's further side one may see you,
As there in a rose-lighted room,
You sit at the window a-thinking,
Half-hid by the flowers in bloom.

Are you tired of the dancing and singing,
The races, the amateur plays,
The breakfasts, and luncheons, and dinners
That fill up these jubilant days?
And you weary of constantly eating
The creamy and cool mayonnaise?

[1] I am sorry the poet used a cockney rhyme.

She might well be—witness the College missioner who came up from South London, and, calling on an old friend, apologized for his bad temper—he had been having all his meals out to meet freshmen, and 'had eaten nothing but salmon mayonnaise for three days'.

What did the Dons say to it all? Let us turn back to an appeal made to them.

> Ye Dons of ancient lore
>   Recall the days of yore,
> And all your solemn state forget awhile.
> Come down to common earth,
>   And let our annual mirth
> Your seemingly steeled hearts again beguile
>   From all that ye pretend that ye
> Prefer to Undergraduate festivity.

What did the Dons make of it? Some were bored—they had seen and heard it all before, and did not always respond to the nieces of their wives—nor want to sit in boats; or they had examination papers to correct. But they too were perhaps still partly human; and, with a soliloquy borrowed from another University magazine, this long-drawn story of undergraduate Cambridge may reach an end.

> The May Week! Yes, and the courts are gay
>   With dresses and hats of the charmingest kind;
> After a winter of work (let us say!)
>   Youth finds the May Week much to its mind.
>
> As I go through the courts in these twilight hours,
>   The rooms lit up with their candle light,
> Girls' voices sound from behind the flowers,
>   Girls' faces look into the summer night.
>
> It does one good such delight to divine
>   In room after room in the candle-glow;
> But I turn to one window that once was mine,
>   And I think of a May Week long ago.

I see her again in the window-seat—
  Her brown hair back in a bunch was tied,
Her voice such a voice! and her smile was sweet;
  And I hoped such hopes—and that year she died.

It was my turn then; it is yours to-day,
  My happy young friend in the room up there,
Love her? Of course! and win—if you may,
  But never think that my life is bare.

But I 'loved and lost'? She died, it is true;
  But 'lost'—ah! that you must never suppose;
What she did for me then, no years undo;
  What she is to me now—my own heart knows.

It's lonely, of course, and life is strange;
  But I think, as on through the courts I go,
My own old sorrow I would not change
  For the cloudless happiness others know.

ENVOY

(From a London paper, now extinct)

'Tis not the Oxonian's somewhat heightened passion
  That thrills our spirits when of thee we dream;
We feel for thee in quite another fashion
      Such as might well beseem
The children of a rather colder clime,
Whose slower blood throbs not to fancy nor in rhyme.

The place—Heav'n help us! 'tis a cheerless region,
  Featureless miles of fen and flat and fen—
And Camus footing slow, amid a legion
      Of sluggish brooks—and then
The yellow brick, all that harsh Nature yields
To build dull rows of streets upon her own dull fields.

Yet take the Northward road, the Roman's planning,
  Via Devana, some time in October;
Heaven lies most strangely open for your scanning,
      And from the dull and sober
East Anglian scene, your eyes seek plains of sky
That wider far and vaster than you dreamed do lie.

Dull is the countryside; but those slow waters,
  Gliding in peace beneath the ancient walls
Founded for God by great Kings and their daughters,
      Chapels and courts and halls,
Keep the grass green; the elms stand, unsurpassed;
And lilac flowers each spring more glorious than the last.

Our grey old Alma Mater runs not riot
  With swift 'great movements', seeks no vague 'wide view';
No! but she puts, in earnest mood and quiet,
      A challenge to be true,
True to the fact, and serious in the quest
Of knowledge; that once gained, content she leaves the rest.

Envoy

Good grey old Mother! quick to curb our fancies
  How I have chafed against thy cautious mood!
And yet, where'er my restless spirit glances,
      I feel thee in my blood,
And, checking, thank kind fortune that my youth
Knew thy controlling hand, thy steady love of truth.

INDEX

CAMBRIDGE: PRINTED BY W. LEWIS, M.A., AT THE UNIVERSITY PRESS

Lightning Source UK Ltd.
Milton Keynes UK
UKOW01f0621040318
318829UK00001B/5/P